The Low-Density University

The Low-Density University

15 Scenarios for Higher Education

Edward J. Maloney and Joshua Kim

With a New Preface

JOHNS HOPKINS UNIVERSITY PRESS

BALTIMORE

Printed in the United States of America on acid-free paper
9 8 7 6 5 4 3 2 1

Johns Hopkins University Press
2715 North Charles Street
Baltimore, Maryland 21218-4363
www.press.jhu.edu

ISBN-13: 978-1-4214-4098-9 (open access)
ISBN-13: 978-1-4214-4097-2 (electronic)
ISBN-13: 978-1-4214-4317-1 (paperback)

Library of Congress Cataloging Control Number: 2021936702

Johns Hopkins University Press uses environmentally friendly book materials, including recycled text paper that is composed of at least 30 percent post-consumer waste, whenever possible.

Contents

Preface to the Paperback Edition

At the time we wrote *The Low-Density University*, the ongoing impact of the COVID-19 pandemic was just beginning to come into focus. Spring 2020 was a period of intense transition, as colleges and universities across the country sent their students home and moved their classes online to maintain instructional continuity. The fall was still months away, but it was becoming increasingly clear that being back on campus, at least at full capacity, was not going to be an option for most schools.

We wrote this book in an attempt to name some of the possibilities for that uncertain fall. To give colleges and universities a range of options that could be mixed and matched in ways that were consistent with the culture, needs, and goals of the individual institutions. Our hope was that schools would make decisions that balanced the health, safety, and well-being of their campus communities but do so in a way that would emphasize the need to be intentional and transparent about the work we were asking of our students and of ourselves as faculty and staff.

Given the specific context in which we wrote this book, one might wonder about its value for the current moment. As we write the preface for this print edition, colleges and universities have been operating under the limitations and conditions of the pandemic for exactly one year. Much like last spring, our understanding of what campuses will look like in fall semester 2021 is still a bit cloudy. We expect schools will be returning to an operating state closer to fall 2019 than to fall 2020. At the same time, we know things will be different from any previous semester. It's likely that social distancing requirements will make reducing density a necessary condition for returning to on-campus instruction in the fall and that the effects of the late stages of the pandemic will require us to adapt our practices in new ways. We hope the models we describe in this book will still prove useful as places to begin a discussion about these necessary adjustments.

Beyond this, though, we believe that the challenges facing colleges and universities will not end with the passing of the pandemic. We hope the ideas in this book will serve as provocations for thinking about how higher education can adapt its curricular and structural models to be responsive to some of the more pressing issues we face, including some that were made even more visible during the past year.

In this regard, COVID-19 has brought into sharp focus some overarching concerns driving the future of higher education. The most prominent (and to our mind most pressing) is the acceleration of a range of structural inequities that determine opportunities and outcomes in the United States. Among these inequities are the persistence of institutional racism and bias, the concentration of wealth, and the extreme levels of political polarization that are one result of unchecked social and economic stratification. The imperative to forthrightly address structural inequities and systemic bias across postsecondary education will (we hope) only grow more acute. Issues of educational equity are tightly coupled with systems of funding, with the cost of government disinvestment in public institutions (particularly community colleges and non-flagship state universities) being borne disproportionately by lower-income and BIPOC (Black, Indigenous, and people of color) students and their families.

This is not the only issue facing higher education in the third decade of the 21st century. Higher education will likely need to contend with extremes of environmental and weather-related events brought on by climate change. The disruptions in early 2021 to basic services such as electricity and clean water following a winter storm in Texas and surrounding states, in addition to cataclysms such as the California wildfires of 2020, are more likely harbingers than exceptions. Beyond equity and climate change, the entire ecosystem of higher education must confront the complex challenges of growing student debt, disinvestment by state and federal governments, demographic shifts, and, perhaps the most disturbing to the fundamental nature of higher education, a growing cultural distrust of information, knowledge, and scholarship. It is with these kinds of challenges in mind that we hope *The Low-Density University* will continue to be useful as we look to the future of higher education. While originally intended to provide a common set of frameworks in the form of 15 scenarios that colleges and universities could utilize to navigate the public health emergency of COVID-19, our hope is that the focus on innovative approaches to investing deeply in student learning can help colleges and universities imagine new ways of thinking about delivering instruction or mapping curriculum.

The scenarios we describe in *The Low-Density University* represent a continuum of non-exclusive options of institutional response to the COVID-19 pandemic. These scenarios are bookended on one side of the continuum by *Back to Normal* and on the other by *Fully Remote*. What has become increasingly clear is that this first scenario of *Back to Normal* is likely to be a *New Normal* as we head into the post-pandemic era. We don't yet know if any of the other scenarios will be adopted in significant ways across higher education, but we expect many colleges and universities will remix and refine all of them as useful for their own contexts. In this respect, the scenarios discussed are all about strategies for maintaining institutional resiliency, and specifically academic continuity, in the face of a pandemic. Resilience and continuity, however, are not concepts exclusive to the institutions. They apply equally as well to the learners whom higher education serves.

To this end, an animating concern that connects each scenario is the impact on educational equity implicit in each option. Because strategies that enable schools to persist in the face of seemingly existential challenges may have the unintended consequence of systemically disadvantaging already disadvantaged groups of students, it's important to keep these challenges always in sight. We attempt to do this in each scenario with a section called *Considerations*, where the focus of each institutional initiative to de-densify the campus is refracted through the lens of equity and access. As campuses re-densify with vaccinated students and faculty and staff who no longer need to be physically distant from one another, the focus on equity and access should become more pressing. By foregrounding the potential unintended effects on equity and access in each of the scenarios discussed in this book, we hope to call attention to the impact of institutional-level strategies as they affect our most vulnerable students. Even as we see the potential for schools to address issues of equity and access by challenging themselves to consider alternative curricular and structural models, we know the desire to get back to a semblance of normal will be strong. This pull could lead many to ignore the lessons of the past year. We hope this will not be the case, as many of the most pressing issues facing higher education can be mitigated through careful design and intentional consideration of the traditions and structures we have imposed upon ourselves.

Higher education may be through the worst consequences of the pandemic. By employing variants of the scenarios discussed in *The Low-Density University*, institutions of higher learning have proven themselves to be among the most resilient of all organizations. It will be what colleges and universities have learned from COVID-19 about educational equity and institutional resilience, and not how our schools operated during the pandemic, that will have the longest-lasting effects on our system of higher education. As such, we hope *The Low-Density University* will be read as a starting place in thinking about the future of higher education after the 2020 COVID-19 pandemic.

The Low-Density University

1. FIFTEEN SCENARIOS

The pandemic caused by COVID-19 is forcing colleges and universities to rethink the entirety of their operations around the health and safety of their students, faculty, and staff. As institutions look to resume residential education, the first questions many schools are asking are "how many students are safe to bring back to campus, when is it safe to do so, and what precautions will we need to take?" Questions about academics, financial stability, operations, sports, and cocurricular activities follow from these questions. Within the context of the COVID-19 pandemic, health and safety are intimately tied to a number of characteristics, including density—or the number of people on campus relative to the physical spaces where students, faculty, and staff live, learn, and congregate—personal and collective safety, and decisions and actions the faculty, staff, and students make as a community.

As those of us living under these conditions have come to understand, social distancing guidelines force us to consider all of these issues as we try to understand how students will learn, how campus cocurricular activities will be carried out, and how the core functions of research and scholarship will continue. The effect of PPE (personal protective equipment, such as face masks) on the ability to actually teach is becoming a more serious consideration as the issues of density are resolved by individual campus decisions. The further students must sit apart from one another in a physical classroom, the lower the number of students that can attend a given face-to-face class session. With these decisions in place, schools are struggling with the best mode of curricular delivery, whether fully remote, in person, or some hybrid of the two.

In writing the fifteen scenarios that appear in this book, our goal was to develop a list of strategies that might prove useful to colleges and universities trying to make sense of the educational and curricular possibilities under what is likely to be the new normal. One way to think of each scenario is as an individual hypothesis for how colleges and universities might approach planning for a future in instruction that is impacted by a dynamic set of health and safety considerations. We first published the original list of fifteen scenarios on the website InsideHigherEd.com on April 22, 2020.[1] Over the three weeks following that, we published a more in-depth description of each scenario. This book brings all of the scenarios together in one place to provide higher education decision-makers a road map for planning for instructional resiliency.

While each scenario stands on its own, the scenarios themselves can be placed on a continuum, bound on one end by *Back to Normal* and the other end by *Fully Remote*. In between these poles are scenarios related to timing (*Late Start*, *Moving Fall to Spring*, and *Structured Gap Year*), student population (*First-Year Intensive* and *Graduate Students Only*), curriculum (*Targeted Curriculum*, *Split Curriculum*, *Block Plan*, and *Modularity*), location (*Students in Residence Learning Virtually* and *Low-Residency*), and instructional method (*HyFlex* and *Modified Tutorial*) (see Figure 1). In conducting research for this book, we've heard from schools about a variety of ways they have used these scenarios. On some campuses, the scenarios served as points of conversation and general ideas about how to approach planning. At other schools, the scenarios were explored one by one, with unlikely scenarios jettisoned while likely scenarios rose to the surface. And at still at other schools, they narrowed the discussion down quickly to two or three scenarios that seemed most likely for their campuses. For many schools, the value of articulating the scenarios in their planning was in giving a name to the plans they were already considering. For others, it introduced some complexity to their thinking.

The interesting thing for us is just how different each school's response has been in planning for educational continuity. In some cases, it seemed perfectly obvious that a modular approach was the right thing to do, but the

1. Edward J. Maloney and Joshua Kim, "15 Fall Scenarios," *Inside Higher Ed*, April 22, 2020, https://www.insidehighered.com/digital-learning/blogs/learning-innovation/15-fall-scenarios.

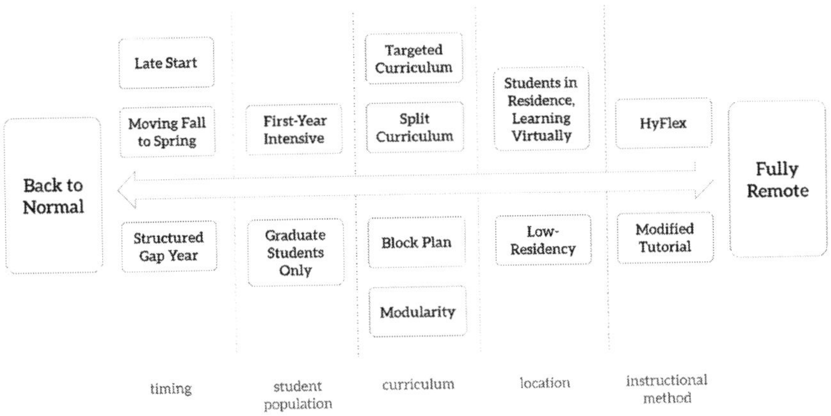

Figure 1

idea of starting late was impossible to imagine. In others, the exact opposite. Starting late seemed the most ethical choice, while modularity seemed far too complicated to imagine pulling off. The novel coronavirus pandemic has highlighted the many common traits all colleges and universities share but also the unique challenges and affordances each place has based on a myriad of factors, from the financial to the geographic to the makeup of their communities to the institutional structures and governances. We also have been hearing about how schools have been working to create their own versions of a combination of scenarios. The scenarios were not intended to be either exhaustive or mutually exclusive. Indeed, it is entirely possible to derive hundreds, if not thousands, of scenarios for what higher education might look like during an ongoing pandemic. Schools interested in modularity may also be considering how a late start would affect the modules, while HyFlex approaches could be designed with first-year students on campuses. The best result for us is the way in which we've heard schools mix, match, and modify the scenarios we describe.

As we dove deeper into each scenario, we tried to be careful to articulate both the reasons why a school might consider that option and why not. Of particular concern for us is the impact of each scenario on student access to, and equity within, a quality postsecondary education. The pivot from residential to remote education has both revealed and amplified the inequalities embedded in the postsecondary system. The degree to which residential education helps bridge these inequalities was clarified by the pandemic-driven cessation of those residential programs. Where equality of educational opportunity never fully existed across the postsecondary ecosystem, it is also true that students from all backgrounds learned and lived in more or less similar circumstances when on campus. Everyone attended class in the same lecture halls, had access to the same academic libraries, and at least as freshmen lived in the same residence halls.

While everyone was learning remotely, the goal that students who attend the same college or university should have a mostly similar educational experience was more difficult to achieve. Students with dedicated access to newer computers, fast and reliable internet connections, and quiet places to study are at a significant advantage. Student-life professionals across the postsecondary ecosystem worked furiously to virtualize the web of academic, social, and psychological supports that have evolved on campuses over the years. Despite their best efforts, however, the speed and scale of shift from residential to online learning have resulted in uneven success. Many students have been left behind. And while the true extent of the level of student disengagement and suboptimal educational outcomes during the weeks and months after the cessation of residential education can't be quantified at this point, anecdotal evidence suggests that it is likely to be severe. At the same time, we are seeing more and more clearly the impact of systemic racism throughout our institutions of higher education. The killings of George Floyd, Ahmaud Arbery, and Breonna Taylor in the spring of 2020 highlighted the complex relationship between colleges and universities with racial injustice.

The challenges of equity, access, and racial injustice run parallel with many other pressures facing higher education. Questions about value, cost, higher education's willingness to change, to evolve, and to adapt have been made more pressing by the crisis of COVID-19, but they are not new. While the fifteen scenarios were meant to give some framework for thinking about a specific challenge facing higher education—COVID-19 in the fall of 2020—we do think many are worth understanding as possible models for academic innovation and transformation well into the future.

As we write this book, many colleges and universities have announced their plans for fall 2020. Most are planning on bringing back some combination of students to campus, either to be taught online or to be taught in some hybrid mode, such as HyFlex or, more and more, a modified tutorial. At the same time, the COVID-19 pandemic has seen a new surge of cases. Spring 2021 is looking more and more like it will parallel, in some form, the fall, with reduced campus density, masks, and remote learning becoming norms across campuses. So, while decisions about the fall have been announced by many schools, most include significant caveats that recognize that the public health concerns may obviate and outweigh any possible decisions made now. It's entirely possible that these choices will be revised given the recent increase in confirmed cases, just as it's possible that the spring will force schools to adopt new approaches to teaching and learning under the conditions of social distancing. We hope these fifteen scenarios will continue to prove useful as a framework for making future decisions.

Scenario #1

Back to Normal

We think any exploration of the range of scenarios for ensuring academic continuity during the COVID-19 pandemic should begin with a baseline. We call this baseline *back to normal*. In many respects, it may seem as if there is little need to write about a return to normal. Wouldn't a return to normal just be the same as all the previous semesters? Perhaps. At some point, our colleges and universities will return as places that do not feature social distancing. There will come a time, sooner or later, when campuses will again be safe places to study, reside, teach, learn, research, and play. But we think things will have changed, too. Even if a combination of COVID-19 testing availability, declines in new diagnoses, and a widely available vaccine make it possible for students, faculty, and staff to gather on our campuses in the same exact way we did in the fall of 2019, *we* will be different. There will be ongoing challenges, lessons learned, and valuable experiences that will impact how we teach and learn. These are all things we think are worth exploring.

For many of us, the sudden interruption of a face-to-face model of higher education revealed just how precious the opportunity to study, teach, live, research, and work on campus is. Students and professors across the country missed the intimacy, immediacy, and human-scale activity that is face-to-face teaching and learning. At the same time, the experience of spring 2020 asked all of us to think more carefully about the range of challenges facing our students, the importance of good teaching, the affordances and problems of technology, the limits and flexibility of our institutional structures and traditions, and the strength of the educational community. A return to normal should necessarily be accompanied by increased attention to each of these issues and more.

If we return to residential teaching and learning, it should be with greater care of our students; a redoubling of our efforts to provide support for the health and well-being of our students, faculty, and staff; a transformed understanding of the important gift of face time with our students; meaningful institutional support for academic advising and mentoring; an investment in the judicious use of technology; a willingness to think creatively and thoughtfully about the institutional structures that support teaching and learning; and a renewed appreciation for the resilience of the campus communities that worked together to make spring 2020 possible. Some of these we highlight below.

Considerations

It has been clear from the early days of COVID-19 that a pandemic magnifies and concentrates academic privilege. Students with abundant resources, including access to computers and fast and reliable bandwidth, enjoy significant advantages over less affluent learners. Vulnerable students may have unstable and chaotic home lives and be exposed to considerable stress as their families bear the financial challenges of a novel virus spread. Institutions have been challenged to extend the system of student support and care that has developed at many residential campuses to the remote learning environment.

Prioritizing educational equity and access is important to all of higher education. There is variation in the success of our institutions in living up to the goal of higher education as an engine of mobility and opportunity, but this is as close to a universally shared value as our sector gets. It is for this reason that the inequalities in equity and access that COVID-19 has both revealed and exacerbated are so painful. The experience of living through a time of educational inequality of opportunities should, we believe, focus our institutions' attention on equity and access once everyone returns to campus. There will be time for students to share their stories of facing the challenges of navigating COVID-19. Exposing the unequal obstacles to succeeding at college, through discussions of the experience of learning in a pandemic, is a necessary step in developing durable and long-lasting structural supports for all learners.

Conversations about universal design for learning will also be more urgent once campus life returns. Unfortunately, higher education as a whole has not matched an investment of resources around universal course design practices with its stated commitments. Ensuring that instructional methods, both residential and online, are accessible to all learners takes preparation, expertise, and resources. Even well-intentioned faculty will have difficulty designing their courses to be accessible to all learners without assistance from accessibility experts and learning designers. The awareness of the struggles that so many students experienced in remote learning will serve to shine a light on the essential work of accessibility and learning design teams. Courses designed around universal design principles will have shown to have had greater success in enabling student success during the pandemic. These practices will likely continue once residential teaching returns.

Moving to virtual learning environments required a quick pivot for all of us. One of the things spring 2020 highlighted for all of us was the need to be flexible. This meant rethinking assignments on fly, adjusting expectations of class time, redefining our learning goals, and adapting experiential and engaged learning to new modalities. This necessary flexibility foregrounded different aspects of our teaching, however, forcing us to look at our content and our assignments in new ways.

That moment also forced us all to learn more about the tools and technologies available to us. While the overnight shift to remote courses was not anyone's idea of a well-planned, -supported, and -executed online learning experience, we've all learned a great deal about what technology can and cannot do. When a return to normal comes, those of us who teach will have much more experience with managing discussions and assignments in Canvas or Blackboard or D2L, and running synchronous online course meetings in Zoom or Hangouts or Teams.

It's conceivable that more faculty will also think differently about the time they are together with students in the classroom. It may take on a new urgency and value. Faculty may attempt to leverage the preciousness of that time together by shifting to recording their lectures on their computers and then asking students to watch before the class meets. This would allow for more meaningful teaching, mentoring, and student research experiences. The tools that made emergency teaching at a distance a reality might be employed to a greater degree to help faculty engage in virtual office hours, manage dynamic peer engagements, and bring in guests from around the world to extend the boundaries of the classroom.

COVID-19 necessitated a move to remote teaching and demonstrated the power of technology to enable academic continuity, but the experience also revealed the limits of technology to catalyze student learning. What matters most in education are the skills and experience of the educator, the level of preparedness and engagement and support of the student, and the degree to which the educational environment is conducive to learning.

When and if we return to a new normal, we hope colleges and universities of all types will engage in sustained conversations about the factors that support or impede student learning. Those conversations, we think, should focus on areas around caring for learners and finding ways to ensure that all courses (independent of course size) contain elements of active and experiential learning. Technology will be part of this conversation as an enabler of student learning, but the limitations of technology will have become clear to the entire campus community.

No doubt a return to normal will bring many changes to our campuses. Social distancing requirements will recede at some point, but we will all need to be prepared to revert back if necessary. Everyone will need to be ready to quickly leave. This awareness of the possibility that the activities of the institution may need to shift at a moment's notice, in part or in whole, to a remote stance is something new in higher education. Knowing this will mean greater attention to what is important about the work we do, the experiences we give our students, and the community we rely on. We expect a return to normal will bring new challenges and new opportunities, many of which will overlap with the other possibilities we see playing out at campuses around the world.

Scenario #2

Late Start

For most campuses, the academic year begins sometime in late August through mid to late September. Given the potential unknowns about the state of the COVID-19 pandemic, including the availability of a vaccine or widespread testing, some colleges and universities looked at ways to shift the increased density of their campuses to a time when we have more resources to support the health, safety, and well-being of our students, faculty, and staff. A *late start* is one option.

Starting late suggests a number of possible approaches, from beginning the semester in earnest at a later time to beginning the semester online at the usual time and then transitioning to an on-campus, face-to-face environment when the global health crisis is more stable. In the case of the former, it could mean attempting to compress the semester into a shorter period (October through December, say) or extending the fall semester into winter and what might normally be the spring semester at many schools. The idea of extending the semester past the normal calendar might mean the suspension of winter breaks as schools attempt to meet the curricular requirements in a reorganized semester.

One advantage of starting late is that it gives colleges and universities a great deal of flexibility, even if pulling off a late start to the semester will require rethinking many of the institutional structures and traditions that define much of college life. Institutional mainstays, such as new student orientation, would need to be reimagined or postponed. Occupancy of residence halls will likely need to shift to later in the semester (or blend into one of many other possible scenarios; see *Students in Residence Learning Virtually*). Beginning the semester early, on the other hand, would allow schools to deliver an entire semester's worth of study before the Thanksgiving break, meaning that our students would not need to travel more than necessary and could finish the semester before a second wave of the pandemic might strike.

If courses were to begin remotely, faculty would be able to engage with students online for a period of time with the expectation that on-campus experiential and hands-on work might happen later in the semester. Students, then, would have an opportunity to build relationships with their faculty and go into the semester with some comfort knowing that their fall semester—for many, their initial experience with college—will continue once the global health crisis is stabilized. Cocurricular activities will continue, albeit at a later time, giving students a key element of the formative and social aspects of college life.

Still, the curriculum and the structure of classes would also likely need to change. Courses might need to run longer to meet seat-time requirements, necessitating changes to course schedules. More courses might need to be fit into a normal week, potentially running courses into the evenings and weekends. Or a blended approach to course delivery might be employed even when students and faculty are on campus. Faculty might use one part of a week to meet with students face-to-face and the other to meet with them online. However we look at it, a late start helps colleges and universities commit to an on-campus experience with students should the health crisis subside. It creates opportunities for a full, rich learning experience for students at the expense of a traditional semester schedule. It does not come without its challenges, however.

Considerations

Starting online and planning to move to face-to-face classes runs the risk of accentuating inequities across student populations. As the forced remote learning weeks of spring 2020 revealed, the pandemic had the effect of magnifying the impact of resources on academic achievement. Those students with access to quiet study environments, fast internet connections, and new computers enjoyed significant advantages over students with fewer of these resources. Vulnerable learners may find themselves starting behind their classmates once the residential portion of the semester begins.

Another challenge to students for a late start plan is, as we've mentioned, first-year orientation. Students accustomed to the expectations and tempo of college-level work may be able to handle the time management and self-motivation necessary to succeed in online courses. First-year students who are both new to college-level work and have likely never learned online may experience more difficulty. Orientation may require a similar rethinking and redesign as courses within the curriculum if a late start is to be successful.

The alternative late-start plan is to announce a later beginning to the residential semester, compressing the remaining time into a more intensive experience. Other options include extending the semester through the December/January winter break, with an October or November start date. If a second wave of COVID-19 should hit, then the late semester start could move from residential to online. The question that many institutions are asking is whether the benefits of a consistent learning modality—residential or online—may outweigh the costs of starting late and going longer.

Transitioning midstream from residential to remote (as in spring 2020), or online to residential, requires a leap in learning behaviors that many students might struggle to master (and possibly reintroduces issues of equity and access for our most vulnerable students). While the future may require rapid transitions from residential to online and back again, depending on the path of the pandemic, institutions will need to develop robust support mechanisms to help their students succeed.

How might a late start look from a faculty and staff perspective? While students would likely be asked to stay away from campus in the late-start model, faculty and staff are another issue. Starting the semester late might mean that faculty and staff return to campus as usual and on time to prepare for the semester, teach from campus, even if online, and engage in research. Having staff return to campus early would allow staff to plan for the complex changes necessary to pull off the late semester.

Or, it may mean that faculty and staff, too, will need to stay home until later in the semester. Our faculty and staff continue to deal with the same family and life challenges that everyone faces. The assumption that they can return to normal while the rest of the campus explores alternatives does not acknowledge the very real stresses of taking care of sick family members, childcare challenges, and the ongoing strain of the pandemic on their lives. Colleges and universities will need to make difficult decisions about the tenure clock, contingent faculty support, and ongoing research support. Whether faculty are on campus or teaching remotely, this time could allow professors to build relationships with their students before seeing them in the lectures hall, seminar rooms, and labs. A focus on interaction, connection, and presence in the online portion of the semester may alleviate some concerns about both course design and student equity.

Like students, faculty will need to rely on institutional support to make starting late a meaningful possibility. Support will need to be in place to help them develop engaging course designs that blend online and face-to-face teaching. The Herculean efforts that were undertaken at most institutions during the spring of 2020 to move courses to a remote learning environment will need to continue. Schools will need to begin working with faculty once the spring semester is over to help them begin preparing for the new normal of teaching and learning under COVID-19. Faculty development, learning design, and technology support will need to be combined to help faculty design course models and approaches to teaching students in blended modes. These designs will need to take advantage of the challenges of the time and space shift in order to make the student experience as dynamic as possible.

Pushing back the date when students, faculty, and staff will return to campus will be appealing to many college and university leaders. The decision to resume residential operations puts a stake in the ground that residential learning will return. Students and parents may be more willing to accept residential delays than a continuation of remote courses. A soft launch of campus operations, perhaps aided by a transitional period of online learning, provides schools with flexibility in the transition back to business as usual. As we have noted, however, there are any number of discernable and hidden costs to pushing back the start of the semester.

Scenario #3

Moving Fall to Spring

As we speak with colleagues from across the country considering different contingencies for institutional resilience, we hear a great deal of nuance to the scenarios we've described. There are complex combinations, extensions, and amendments that build on each school's unique context and signature strengths. Similarly, most schools we speak with are not developing one plan but many. This is prudent. As they put together these contingency plans, every school throughout the country has had to consider a multitude of factors, including the health and safety of their students, faculty, and staff as well as the advice, guidance, and restrictions imposed by their local and state governments. They have had to consider the makeup of their student body, the implications of any scenario for giving students the richest possible learning experience, and the pedagogical approaches most likely to succeed.

Research-heavy schools think specifically about the impact of any one scenario on research and scholarship, not to mention promotion and tenure and the capacity of their faculty. Hopefully, they also consider the well-being of their nontenure line and contingent faculty. These are some of the most vulnerable members of our communities. Any scenario under discussion needs to bear in mind the administrative and operational structures in place to support a given scenario. And, of course, schools have no choice but to consider the financial impact of any given contingency plan. This brings us to our third scenario, *moving fall to spring*.

As with the previous two scenarios, moving the fall semester to a spring start addresses this issue of campus density by considering alternative approaches to the traditional academic calendar. It is a time-based plan. This scenario is perhaps the easiest to describe while at the same time being one of the most difficult to choose. The assumption behind this scenario is that a school would skip the fall semester entirely and begin face-to-face instruction in January 2021. Among many reasons, a school might choose to pause until the spring for health and safety reasons alone, believing that the extra few months will bring with them increased testing and perhaps even signs of a vaccine. They might choose this path because they do not have the infrastructure to support robust remote course delivery. They might choose this path because they believe social distancing would be impossible to manage effectively on a densely populated campus. They might choose this path because they believe it would give them more time to prepare the campus for a potential second wave. Or they might choose this path because they are concerned about inequities among their students' access to the necessary technology, space, and safety required for attentive online learning. Likely, the choice to move the fall semester to the spring would be made based on a combination of these and many other reasons.

The challenges of such a choice are at the very least academic and financial. Skipping the fall means progress toward a degree is lost. Students' first-year experience would be postponed and possibly shortened, while students in need of campus support services might have difficulty receiving them if any were offered. Much like the late-start scenario, starting school in January does not necessarily mean that faculty and staff could not return to campus to prepare for the spring, maintain research continuity, and help support students from afar. But how would schools pay for this time? Losing a semester's worth of tuition at a time when most schools are already struggling because of the financial hit from spring 2020 is a very difficult proposition. Few have massive endowments with cash flexibility. Lost revenue from residence halls and other on-campus activities is a problem in many of the scenarios we outline. Losing a semester's worth of tuition as well is very difficult to imagine given already tight budgets.

These challenges might be mitigated by trying to compress the fall, spring, and summer semesters into eight packed months starting in the spring and running through August. Still, for a variety of reasons, this may not be not ideal. Schools would need to have enough financial flexibility to pay their bills, students would have a semester with nothing planned to do, and faculty and staff would be working in relative uncertainty. Students who need the greatest support might be asked to accelerate their studies in ways that are unmanageable. None of these are good choices, but this is a time of increasingly difficult choices, and finding the option that resonates with the factors each individual school is considering is necessary.

Considerations

For schools choosing this path, we think it will be crucial to make resources available to support our most vulnerable students, faculty, and staff. This is not a consideration unique to this scenario, but a full semester away from campus places this challenge in stark relief. With unemployment likely to remain high throughout the pandemic, it will be difficult for our students to find work as an alternative to staying enrolled in school. Students with the greatest needs while on campus will also need support while off campus, even if the semester is on hold.

How this will happen at each school will depend on the resources, culture, and context of the school. Will it be possible to ask students to propose a project for the semester? Will they receive ongoing support from health and counseling services? Will the timing of financial aid packages shift? Will international students be able to adjust their visas? These are only a few of the questions that schools would struggle with if they decided to go this route. Decreasing density on campus for a semester might not preclude faculty returning to campus to perform research and scholarship. Still, since campus-based research often involves student support, not having students on campus may slow down significant portions of research. Promotion and tenure clocks will likely need to be reconsidered. Many faculty and staff will, like spring 2020, be balancing complex home lives within an economic and social environment that might mean daycare and family care options are also shut down. A January start might give them time to prepare for classes.

If a school does pursue this approach, we believe it will also be crucial for them to consider the plight of contingent faculty and graduate students serving as teaching associates. Many of our adjuncts and lecturers depend on piecing together four or five courses a semester to make ends meet. Our graduate students will have similar issues. Their stipends support their living expenses. One possibility would be to employ our contingent faculty and graduate students to help the rest of the campus prepare for the January start, working alongside colleagues to prepare classes and online materials. But this option depends heavily on available funds, something likely to be a challenge at most institutions. There are few perfect options for the colleges and universities designing contingency plans.

All of the available options have tradeoffs and will force difficult decisions. The idea of starting the academic year in January highlights just how complex managing this will be.

Scenario #4

First-Year Intensive

Under the *first-year intensive* scenario, only first-year students would be invited to begin the academic year on campus. Sophomores, juniors, and seniors would continue to live and study at a distance. Choices around graduate and professional students might be made separately, as these older learners are likely to live off campus and have smaller classes and therefore pose a completely separate challenge in plans for limiting campus density.

The first-year experience privileges one of the most important aspects of college for those institutions that provide a residential educational experience for newly minted high school graduates. While a minority of students new to higher education are able to enjoy a campus-based living and learning experience, as the plurality of students are now nontraditional in age and circumstances, freshman year remains disproportionately important across the spectrum of residential institutions.[2]

The rationale for a first-year intensive plan is found in its name—the first year of college is intense. First-year orientation programs are critical in acclimating new students to the academic rigors of college life as well as to the pitfalls possible in the newfound freedoms of living and studying away from home. For many emerging adults new to the demands of college-level work, it is the first week and months of freshman year that lay the foundations for a successful college career. This is true, too, for the students

2. "Today's Students," Lumina Foundation, accessed May 29, 2020, https://luminafoundation.org/wp-content/uploads/2019/02/todays-student.pdf.

historically categorized as "nontraditional." These students are often starting (or returning to) school while balancing families and full-time work. The first-year experience could help acclimate them to college work and college life as well.

The resources that residential institutions have invested in first-year orientation programs have been dramatically increased in recent years. At most institutions, special care is now taken in the intentional building of community and support networks. Individual counseling, planned events, and other resources have been directed toward underrepresented populations and other specific groups, such as first-generation and LGBTQ students. This support is perhaps more important now in this period of uncertainty.

For schools, committing to bringing first-year students to campus for as close to a traditional freshman experience as possible may have the advantage of attenuating the anticipated matriculation melt. For many newly entering college students (and their parents), the likely dislocations of a fully or partially remote academic year enhance the appeal of a gap year. The perceived opportunity costs of taking a year off from school between high school and college seem to be less at the start of a college career than in the middle. Pre-COVID-19, the idea that many students would benefit from a gap year before starting college was a commonly expressed sentiment and was not discouraged by institutions of higher learning.[3]

As the pandemic plays out, uncertainty about the value of a first-year experience during a time of social distancing may cause a dramatic increase in students choosing to defer enrollment. For tuition-dependent institutions, big jumps in the number of accepted students choosing to matriculate at a later date could result in significant financial hardship. Large drops in the number of first-year students would scramble the budgets of even relatively well-resourced institutions. A first-year intensive strategy may go some distance in ameliorating the concerns of new college students and their parents and may discourage many from choosing to delay the start of their college careers. Whether or not continuing remote classes will cause large numbers of women and men who are further along in their college

3. Joe O'Shea, "Don't Go to College Next Year," *Inside Higher Ed*, January 16, 2014, https://www.insidehighered.com/views/2014/01/16/more-students-should-take-gap-years-going-college-essay.

careers to take a semester off—while perhaps taking online classes at less expensive community colleges—is unknown.

Down the road, the advantages of bringing first-year students to campus may pay off in attrition and retention.[4] For all but the most selective institutions, four- and six-year graduation rates remain atrociously low, and over a third of students may choose to transfer to another school.[5] The potential impacts on time to graduation and retention from having first-year students begin their college careers as remote learners are unknown. We know that the support and community-building structures that have evolved over decades for first-year residential students are difficult to translate to remote learners without significant resources.

Considerations

If schools decide to follow a first-year intensive plan, what might an academic year look like for all students? For first-year students, the start of college is likely to be very different than the traditional freshman experience. The enforced personal growth of adapting to living in a dorm room with a stranger (or two) is likely not to exist for this entering class, as likely all rooms will be singles. Perhaps first-year students will not see this change as a loss. Other differences may be more jarring. A semester with only first-year students in residence means no sporting events to attend since social distancing rules will delay any gatherings with large crowds regardless of the school's plan to de-densify the campus. At schools where fraternities and sororities play a big role in the campus social scene, alternatives will need to be discovered. Dining halls may be open, but students may be required to eat in shifts or perhaps grab their meals to go.

Having first-year students come to campus to live and to study does not necessarily mean that all, or even most, classes will be face-to-face. First-year students would likely be asked to enroll in a combination of residential and online courses. Large-enrollment gateway courses may need to shift to online teaching, as packed lecture halls are unlikely to conform to social

4. "Fast Facts: Graduation Rates," National Center for Education Statistics, accessed May 30, 2020, https://nces.ed.gov/fastfacts/display.asp?id=40.

5. Valerie Strauss, "Why So Many College Students Decide to Transfer," *Washington Post*, January 29, 2017, https://www.washingtonpost.com/news/answer-sheet/wp/2017/01/29/why-so-many-college-students-decide-to-transfer.

distancing guidelines. Normally, most college courses contain a mix of students at different places in their college careers. Even in a first-year intensive strategy, first-year students would join their sophomore, junior, and senior peers in online classes. The risk to older faculty of contact with young people may result in first-year students learning on campus from faculty who are remote.

A first-year intensive strategy also raises any number of questions and concerns about equity and access. How feasible is it to expect that undergraduates who have had to navigate a spring and a summer of remote courses to continue on this path? As we have pointed out in our discussions of the three previous scenarios, remote learning tends to concentrate student privilege while further disadvantaging vulnerable learners. Bringing only first-year students to campus might deepen structural inequalities of opportunity. Continuing remote learning for sophomores, juniors, and seniors may also make it more difficult for these students to progress toward graduation. Courses with heavy lab components and other forms of hands-on instruction remain challenging to transition online. First-year students may benefit most from the orientation activities and development of social networks that campus life encourages, but they may need physical classrooms less than their further-along peers.

For professors and staff, a first-year intensive start to the academic year would still mean the additional challenge of developing both residential and remote courses. Student (and parent) expectations for the quality of remote courses are likely to be significantly higher than were expectations in spring 2020. During that emergency pivot, schools were careful to label courses as *remote* rather than *online*, as online courses carry with them expectations of advanced course design and significant investments in faculty training. Students (and parents) may expect that courses offer *no significant difference* in quality between residential and online delivery modes. They will likely be less patient about variation in course design and methods of delivery. A first-year intensive plan may make it difficult for faculty, and the staff they work with, to develop and teach high-quality online courses while simultaneously developing and teaching their face-to-face courses.

However, this strategy would also potentially allow for greater resources to be allocated to first-year academic experiences, such as first-year seminars and experiential learning activities. Faculty could potentially invest more time in mentoring first-year students, building relationships that could last for a student's entire time at an institution. As with all the scenarios we discuss in this series, every choice to begin the fall semester in the low-density university has serious drawbacks. Bringing first-year students to campus has many advantages for both students and schools, but downsides are considerable. Communicating the rationale for this plan to all stakeholders is essential. These communications should be open about the rationale for adopting this strategy, while transparently addressing its shortcomings and difficulties. Finding ways to keep residential and remote learners together as a cohesive community will occupy much of the time and energy of campus leaders.

Scenario #5

Graduate Students Only

Much like the previous scenario, having only graduate students on campus reduces density by selectively allowing certain students to return to campus. There are many possible approaches to selecting which students might be allowed to return to campus and which would be asked to learn remotely. Colleges might choose to bring to campus students who are the most vulnerable and need the greatest support, students who are in certain schools or disciplines, students in certain classes, and so on. While a first-year intensive approaches the issue of density by focusing on the all-important first-year experience, *graduate students only* prioritizes the benefits of bringing a distinct group of advanced students back to campus.

At schools with a sizable graduate student population, a graduate students only approach to meeting the needs of reducing the density of campus has a number of advantages. The first is that bringing back only graduate students to campus solves one of the more vexing challenges of residential education under social distancing—the residence hall. While it is true that many graduate students live in university-provided residences, these units almost always differ from the dorms that house most undergraduates. Most university-provided graduate student housing consists of singles, suites, or apartments. On residential campuses with graduate programs, a higher proportion of graduate students live off campus than do undergraduates. If university-provided graduate housing is still too dense, then graduate students could occupy the rooms of undergraduates who are studying online.

A second advantage of following a graduate students only path has to do with research. While library research can more and more be conducted online, graduate students in the humanities often still need access to special collections and unique on-campus resources. Even more complicated are graduate students in STEM fields who often require labs for their work. Progressing toward completion of the degree means conducting experiments. Graduate students often work to support faculty research as well. Graduate students also help conduct research on grant-funded projects out of faculty labs that require access to specialized equipment. While it is possible (if challenging) to move undergraduate STEM instruction from physical to virtual labs—shifting from atoms to bits as teaching tools—it is much more difficult to imagine original research of a similar kind happening online. Simulations may work well for learning, but we are not yet at the point where all graduate student research can be virtualized. It is often a hands-on enterprise. Having graduate students return to campus helps address this issue.

The third benefit of graduate students only might be the positive impact that this plan could have on undergraduate instruction. One of the big lessons of higher education's emergency pivot to remote instruction has been that the rate limiters to quality student learning experiences have less to do with technology and more to do with people. Remote learning is massively labor-intensive. Moving instruction to digital platforms heightens, rather than diminishes, the need for complementary faculty resources such as teaching assistants. The biggest single predictor of a successful online course is instructor presence. Having course assistants to distribute the grading and student engagement to frees professors up for high-value activities such as coaching, mentoring, and just-in-time content creation.

If funding is available, graduate students (who are not themselves teachers of record in a course) could be asked to help support remote instruction for other faculty, including other graduate student teachers. This would not only benefit the ongoing university instruction but it would be an invaluable experience for graduate students as future teachers. Participating as educators in online courses would provide graduate students with marketable skills, both in and out of academia.

Considerations

If graduate students only carries with it a number of advantages—no need to worry about social distancing in large lecture classes since the largest of the professional school classes could likely relocate comfortably to the largest undergraduate lecture halls; less worry about violating social distance guidelines at parties and social events, as graduate students have smaller parties and are (on the whole) less social; additional assistance in getting faculty research restarted, to the extent that graduate students are inexpensive and indispensable research labor—what are the challenges with this approach? Perhaps the most obvious is that many schools do not have significant graduate student populations. This is both a positive and negative. Smaller graduate student populations would contribute significantly toward reduced density on campus, but for many schools, the population would not be large enough to help support undergraduate teaching or faculty research.

Another consideration is housing. On campuses with larger graduate student populations, bringing graduate students back to campus would help reduce density in residence halls and would mean a university would have less to do to manage the social distancing of students living on campus. The variability of graduate student housing does pose two problems, however. First, for many residential campuses, revenue from renting dormitory rooms is a significant source of revenue. Graduate students tend to live off campus and would not help universities recuperate this lost revenue. Second, if a graduate student becomes sick, it becomes much more difficult for the college to trace contacts and to quarantine the student. A single graduate student could end up creating problems for managing the spread of an outbreak on campus.

A third problem with the graduate students only approach may simply be that colleges and universities already know how to create immersive, rich, and intensive low-residency and online graduate programs. Indeed, outside of the most selective residential professional degree programs, the trend has been for master's programs to transition from residential to online.[6] Why bring back the students who are best able to adapt their work to online learning? What colleges and universities have not figured out how to do, outside small experiments such as Minerva, is to replicate the residential

6. Scott Jaschik, "Illinois Will End Residential M.B.A.," *Inside Higher Ed*, May 28,

undergraduate experience online. The traditional undergraduate bundle has been difficult to disrupt not because of its instructional aspects but because of its social attributes. This is why the plan at Southern New Hampshire University (SNHU) to give undergraduates the option to live in residence halls and take classes online is so fascinating.[7] The press stories about SNHU's plans unsurprisingly focused on the waiving of tuition, but the real long-term story is SNHU's move to use its campus for social learning while seeking to leverage online learning to lower overall costs.

Bringing only graduate students back to campus, then, may not address some of the more palpable existential worries of starting a new academic year amid the uncertainty of the pandemic's progression. We don't know what the public health situation will be going forward, but offering a campus-based experience to undergraduates is a key value proposition of predominantly residential institutions.[8] The graduate students only scenario is likely to be little more than a thought experiment in solving the puzzle of reducing the density on campus. Exploring this option illuminates how complex the situation is and how important it is for colleges and universities to think about all possible options. It also foregrounds just how important a campus option for undergraduates is to the future of residential colleges and universities.

2019, https://www.insidehighered.com/quicktakes/2019/05/28/illinois-will-end-residential-mba.

7. Southern New Hampshire University, "Southern New Hampshire University Sets Out to Reimagine Campus-Based Learning, Offers Full Tuition Scholarships for Incoming Freshmen," press release, accessed May 30, 2020, https://www.snhu.edu/about-us/newsroom/2020/04/full-tuition-scholarships-for-incoming-freshmen.

8. Christina Paxson, "College Campuses Must Reopen in the Fall. Here's How We Do It," *New York Times*, April 26, 2020, https://www.nytimes.com/2020/04/26/opinion/coronavirus-colleges-universities.html.

Scenario #6

Structured Gap Year

One of the most prevalent questions parents and high school seniors have been asking about academic offerings under the conditions prompted by COVID-19 is whether they should avoid the challenges altogether and take a gap year? The sixth of fifteen scenarios we suggest as worth considering for conditions under COVID-19 and for future academic transformation is for schools to consider offering the option of a *structured gap year*.

Creating or augmenting institutional infrastructure designed to enable and support admitted and matriculated students in a gap year may be a difficult choice for many colleges and universities to make. A gap year is a year in which no tuition or fees are collected from the students engaged in this option. Taking a gap year means that a college or university will hold a place for the student, ensuring reentry into the institution in the following year. Institutions are scrambling to develop plans that will encourage students to matriculate, while also figuring out how to work around social distancing guidelines that are likely to be strict. Taking steps to actively decrease enrollment, such as developing plans to widely roll out a structured gap year, may appear to be counter to the financial interests of most schools even while offering other advantages worth considering.

Students and their parents understand that higher education during COVID-19 will almost certainly be different than previous years, and certainly different than what they might imagine college life to be. That will likely be the case for all of us. A gap year for entering freshman has long been understood as advantageous for students' later academic success.[9] The overriding goal for any gap year plan is that the experience is meaningful, ideally leading to greater levels of maturity, independence, and confidence.[10]

With little likelihood that students will be able to spend the 2020–2021 academic year living outside their home country, or participating in service projects or place-based educational programs, what might a structured gap year program look like? One possibility is for colleges and universities to provide students some structure for a productive year away from campus and classes while keeping the costs for providing these resources commensurate with revenues. The structured gap year, therefore, could exist along a continuum, with some student costs for activities that involve more significant efforts by professors and staff, and less costly or no charges for activities that require little to no marginal·outlays by institutions.

Schools could establish independent research projects that students undertake with the guidance of a professor, and maybe a cohort of other students. Creative research projects that are amenable to being completed while living at home might be more attractive to some students than enrolling in remote courses, or of even managing the uncertainty of when a return to campus might be possible. The greater the involvement of the school and professors in a structured gap year project, the more room there is to maintain a student's association with the school. At the far end of the spectrum are credit-eligible projects, which can be evaluated by faculty and charged at the going credit-hour rate.

Independent or small cohort research projects may work for some students in a structured gap year scenario, but not all. Some students would be challenged to develop the discipline needed to complete a large project, lacking the incentives and nudges of a class schedule, regular assessments, and grades. An alternative option for students in this scenario who are unable to either work (as the employment situation is as fragile as the residential campus situation) or live outside of their homes would be to act as course assistants. Normally, course assistants are drawn from graduate

9. "Gap Year Data & Benefits," Gap Year Association, accessed on May 30, 2020, https://www.gapyearassociation.org/data-benefits.php.

10. Robert Farrington, "Here's Every Reason You Should Take a Gap Year before College," *Forbes*, June 10, 2019, https://www.forbes.com/sites/robertfarrington/2019/06/10/heres-every-reason-you-should-take-a-gap-year-before-college.

students, or in some cases advanced undergraduates as teaching assistants. We are not in normal times, and this new normal could lead to transformative practices that extend well beyond the present moment. To accomplish this approach, therefore, schools could develop online training programs to instill the skills that course assistants need to add value to classes. There are many examples of students acting as peer mentors and learning fellows, a methodology that has proven to be highly successful. Recalibrating these programs to train and deploy even incoming first-year students may prove equally successful.

As schools rely more heavily on virtual instruction, the availability of students to serve in peer mentoring roles, or to even handle some of the elements of digital instruction (video editing, helping with device troubleshooting) may prove invaluable. Course assistants would be there not to grade assignments or exams but to assist in supporting the learning of others, a task that may feel both meaningful and accomplishable for students who want to hold off on taking their own classes. Compensation could be in the form of credit, helping students build or maintain momentum toward matriculation and graduation.

Considerations

Designing opportunities for independent research projects and course assistants are just two of the potential ideas of the structured gap year. Exploring the awarding of credit absent the requirement of matriculation may free schools up to be creative with student projects and peer engagement. For students (and their parents) a structured gap year program has the potential advantage of keeping rising and existing learners involved in meaningful tasks, activities that should improve the odds of successfully navigating a college career. At the same time, the continuum of possible offerings this scenario, with costs tied to faculty/school involvement and credit, may allow for significant savings in tuition and fees as compared to full enrollment.

For schools, the advantage of investing in the infrastructure necessary to offer a structured gap year experience would be twofold. First, reducing the size of the matriculating student body might go some way in enabling other students to return to campus. Fewer students mean more space in residence halls, dining facilities, classrooms, libraries, and labs. As the overwhelming imperative is for residential institutions to offer campus-based options, any plan that allows students to gracefully self-sort time away from campus may prove helpful.

The second advantage for colleges and universities of investing in standing up and running a structured gap year program may be in the potential of this option to keep students integrated with their school. The alternative of students and their families planning a gap year that is disconnected from the institution is arguably worse than offering an institutionally integrated gap year. And, third, colleges and universities could design a gap year experience that is more equitable and accessible for all students. The practice of the gap year has often been criticized as a luxury available only to the wealthy.[11] The likely need to de-densify campuses may perhaps offer an opportunity for institutions to democratize the gap year experience by offering students a richer and more institutionally integrated set of options under this scenario. Schools could create the scaffolding and infrastructure to make a gap year a viable possibility for students for whom this would otherwise be unrealizable.

One possible outcome is that the gap year evolves into a *visiting year*, with homebound students taking classes at community colleges with the goal of transferring less-expensive credits to more expensive residential institutions.[12] This plan may prove attractive for some. A structured gap year offers an alternative for students and their families who may be unwilling or unable to pay retail prices for what they see as a different educational experience but who want to stay connected to their schools while progressing toward a degree.

Much like many of the scenarios we have been discussing, a structured gap year may be more of a thought experiment at most institutions than a fully implementable plan. It may be something that could be made available to a small number of students, or it could simply force schools to consider the advantages of a gap year for all students. This would not be a bad result.

The COVID-19 pandemic is a difficult and challenging moment for all of higher education, but it also has shone a light on so many of the inequities

11. Vikram Barhat, "Is Gap-Year Volunteering a Luxury for the Rich?," *BBC Worklife*, July 16, 2016, https://www.bbc.com/worklife/article/20160714-is-gap-year-volunteering-a-luxury-for-the-rich.

12. Matt Reed, "The 'Visiting Year,'" *Inside Higher Ed*, April 28, 2020, https://www.insidehighered.com/blogs/confessions-community-college-dean/%E2%80%98visiting-year%E2%80%99.

and challenges facing our students. Access to the internet, reliable technology, and a safe workspace are only some of the immense challenges many of our students face. Thinking through the advantages and challenges of a structured gap year during COVID-19 highlights the financial and practical difficulty many of our students would have in taking advantage of this kind of meaningful experience.

Scenario #7

Targeted Curriculum

Developing a *targeted curriculum* enables campus social distancing through a strategic design of face-to-face and online course offerings and schedules. In a targeted curriculum, certain courses are designated as high priority, are provided with institutional resources, and may be given precedence for being taught on campus. For example, courses with high demand but capped enrollments, such as seminars, might be taught on campus, as might courses that are essential to allow students to fulfill graduation requirements. Similarly, experiential courses, performance-based courses, and labs might be given priority for on-campus meetings, as might courses that require intense faculty-student feedback and discussion, such as writing courses and first-year seminars.

What "priority" means will vary from school to school. Some schools may give additional resources to courses designated as high priority, such as learning designers and teaching assistants. For others, it might simply mean they are designated to be taught on campus or even taught at all during a semester of limited resources. Deciding on the priority of certain courses over others might mean that courses with unintentionally low enrollments are either taught online or more likely not offered at all. At the other end of the class-size spectrum, large-enrollment gateway courses could either be taught online or divided into smaller sections that would be taught on campus in classrooms freed up by moving other courses online. To account for these changes, faculty used to teaching upper-division electives and seminars might be asked instead to teach face-to-face versions of the now divided up large-enrollment gateway courses. Things would have to change at all levels for a targeted curriculum to work.

Whatever the choices, a targeted curriculum path requires that the schools and departments within the university design the course offerings as a cohesive plan, working within constraints of student needs, pedagogical opportunities, and social distancing guidelines. On the student need side, developing a targeted curriculum plan might involve careful effort to offer courses on campus that enhance the likelihood of student success while also ensuring that university-wide and major requirements can be satisfied. Students, particularly students wishing to major in STEM, are at greatest risk of falling off the path to a degree while attempting to progress through foundational courses. First-generation and underrepresented minority students in STEM majors are at particularly high risks for attrition.[13]

A targeted curriculum plan would to some degree indicate that the college or university believes that all students do not succeed equally in residential and online classes. Students who are advanced in their majors might find online courses manageable, as these learners have presumably developed the foundational knowledge, study skills, and time management abilities that are critical for online learning success. Students new to a subject or a major, as well as those who are still finding their higher ed sea legs, might benefit more from the defined structures and visibility inherent in face-to-face courses.

This is not to say that introductory or gateway courses can't be taught well online, but rather that doing so is highly resource-intensive and may not be possible at many institutions, particularly at the scale and speed necessary to be ready for the start of the new academic year. Planning to run gateway courses as face-to-face classes, and doing so by spreading out students across sections and classrooms, has the added benefit of creating smaller student-to-faculty ratios—a change that might yield significant benefits in student outcomes.

A targeted curriculum could also begin to address the challenge of running lab, performance-based, and experience-intensive courses as well. Committing to offer these courses—or a part of these courses—as

13. Alan Green and Danielle Sanderson, "The Roots of STEM Achievement: An Analysis of Persistence and Attainment in STEM Majors," *American Economist* 63, no. 1 (2017): 79–93, https://doi.org/10.1177/0569434517721770.

face-to-face offerings avoids the challenges of virtualizing labs and adapting experiential and performance-based studies to an online modality. At the same time, it would allow the school to suspend low-enrollment courses and move electives online. Reducing the overall number of residential courses based on student needs, pedagogical goals, and social distancing requirements could also create more space in schedules to offer residential courses that have hands-on and laboratory components.

Considerations

Thinking through a targeted curriculum scenario is challenging because the curricular facts on the ground vary so widely across the higher education ecosystem. Each school has some combination of student needs and course offerings that is unique to its circumstances. Each school seemingly has its own wrinkles in faculty governance, major and graduation requirements, and instructional practices. At most schools, the courses offered in any single semester result from the interplay of various forces, incentives, guidelines, rules, structures, requirements, and preferences. The courses that faculty are assigned to teach result from a combination of structure and of agency, with *some* professors having *some* degree of voice in determining their courses.

Under a targeted curriculum, course offerings would likely need to be coordinated across the institution rather than at the level of the department or school. The schedule of courses would be holistically designed around the requirements of reducing density, with attention to student needs and pedagogical best practices. The end result might be more faculty teaching core, introductory, and required courses, with a commensurate decline in the number of electives on offer.

A targeted curriculum would also need to be developed in the context of classroom availability. Decreasing the number of low-demand/low-enrollment residential courses (by moving these courses online or to not running) would open up classroom space to spread other courses out. Unless a university has an amazing surfeit of classroom space, however, moving some courses online will likely not be enough to ensure a student and faculty classroom density that is low enough to meet social distancing guidelines. Classroom utilization will also need to increase, with more face-to-face classes offered in the early morning, during evenings, and perhaps on weekends.

Increasing the number of professors assigned to high-demand/high-enrollment residential courses might also mean that more faculty could teach in teams. Many introductory courses already share a common curriculum, textbooks, lecture materials, and exams. Teams of professors, hopefully augmented by both learning designers and teaching assistants, could work together to prepare and manage sections. This collaboration could have significant benefits for students in a time of greater need for attention, care, and mentoring. Unfortunately, a targeted curriculum does not solve the challenge of where students live under the requirements of a low-density university. It is possible, if likely difficult, to spread students out across classrooms. Space in residence halls may prove less fungible than space in residential classrooms. There is no online option for a bed. Schools may move students into hotel rooms in order to maintain residential social distancing.

For many schools, a targeted curriculum would likely be part of a larger set of considerations. Do they bring all their students back to live in dorms? Only some? Are courses not prioritized taught online or not at all? Any consideration of a targeted curriculum, however, should not just be exclusively taken with an eye toward managing the teaching and learning during the pandemic, but rather it should consider the potential effects on the future of the entire curriculum at that institution. A worst-case scenario is for courses not given priority under the current crisis to be considered somehow less valuable than other courses, determinations that should rightly be made at the department and school level. Such courses might be mistaken to have less value to an institution and be left out of the curriculum for longer than intended. This would mean long-term curricular decisions were made in haste and without full consideration. The variety of academic experiences that students come to expect as part of a college degree could be unintentionally diminished without careful curation of a targeted curriculum.

Scenario #8

Split Curriculum

In a *split curriculum*, courses are designated as *either* residential or online. Scheduled face-to-face courses are optimized for maximum classroom utilization under conditions of social distancing. Careful thought is given to which courses work best for students when taught face-to-face and which courses are more amenable to online delivery methods. A split curriculum has many of the advantages of a targeted curriculum in that schools can make proactive choices about which courses to offer to maximize student success. The main difference between these two strategies is that a targeted curriculum would likely result in fewer courses being offered as faculty are redeployed around high-demand/high-impact courses. A split curriculum seeks to preserve as much of the full catalog as possible by distributing courses across residential and online options.

Organizing classes under a split curriculum has a number of advantages. For students, this plan maximizes the number of potential face-to-face courses in which they are eligible to enroll. Courses that are likely to be especially beneficial for students if run face-to-face can be prioritized for classroom space. Some students may prefer a residential learning experience for introductory and other foundational courses. Other students, even those living on or close to campus, may instead prefer the flexibility of online learning. Depending on how it's implemented, a split curriculum could offer students the option of being able to choose the course delivery method that best meets their needs.

For faculty, a split curriculum has the advantage of narrowing the course design and delivery process to a single modality. Professors would be able to plan their courses as *either* residential or remote. As expectations rise for online course quality as virtual learning becomes the new normal, faculty require more time and assistance to develop quality online courses. A split curriculum clearly delineates residential courses from online courses, enabling both professors and schools to focus time and resources into course development and delivery. Faculty preferences for teaching in a classroom or remotely can be taken into account in the development of the schedule, though we imagine this will be a difficult negotiation regardless. For faculty who are concerned about potential health risks in teaching on campus, a split curriculum can accommodate their preferences for teaching online.

Among the most significant concerns colleges and universities are facing is the worry that students may end up deferring if the semester is taught under social distancing conditions. The in-person portion of the college experience is a crucial value for residential institutions. Layered on the potential loss of the full campus experience may be a diminishing willingness among students (and their parents) to pay residential-level tuitions for a remote-learning education. The understanding and patience students had with the initial shift to emergency remote instruction in spring 2020 is rightly being replaced with an expectation of high-quality courses, regardless of their modality. This means online courses that are designed around established instructional design principles, that are consistent in quality, and that prioritize student engagement and faculty presence.

A split curriculum would attempt to address at least some of the concerns of students and their parents. By choosing this approach, colleges and universities would be committing to online as part of a strategy, rather than as a last resort. To achieve this, faculty development and instructional design resources would need to be made available to all faculty teaching a remote course. Faculty would need to commit to adapting their courses to an online mode rather than attempting to translate existing courses to a new space in a pinch. And students would need to be given support and resources to make the online component a rich part of their educational experience. Universities would be able to provide a rich, if split, residential experience and they will be able to point to institutional investment in quality online courses. Schools previously unwilling to see their undergraduate curriculum taught online were in spring 2020 running *both* residential and online operations at the undergraduate level. The split curriculum is in many respects an acknowledgment that we are in a new normal.

Considerations

The challenges of split curriculum are (at least) threefold. The first challenge—one that runs across all of the scenarios—is student housing. Every scenario that includes face-to-face classes must first answer the question, where will the students live? Social distancing guidelines make it difficult to imagine students living in doubles or triples, while a student in a residence hall exposed to the virus would likely need to be quarantined. These will be difficult operational challenges from a public health, legal, and logistical standpoint. Some colleges and universities may be able to sign semester-length leases with local hotels. Of all the challenges of the low-density university, student housing may be the most vexing.

If the student housing puzzle can be solved, however, colleges and universities may be in a good position to provide a quality (if different) learning experience. Despite long-standing assumptions about the inability of higher education to change, one of its great strengths is the ability of individual institutions to rapidly evolve and adapt to new circumstances. That every institution was able to quickly pivot in a matter of days from residential to remote learning in March 2020 as the COVID-19 pandemic unfolded is testimony to the resilience of higher education. In contrast to other industries, and even other sectors within education such as K-12, higher education was able to maintain academic and business continuity at an unmatched speed and scale.

Moving to a split curriculum may be the next step in higher education resilience under the demands of social distancing and pandemic preparation. This step and the second challenge, however, is likely to be organizationally difficult and resource-intensive. A split curriculum would likely require colleges and universities to develop parallel operations to support both residential and online learning programs. For large residential institutions, the scale on which undergraduate online courses must be designed and run is far beyond anything experienced or even contemplated in the past.

Even if schools are able to maximize the number of face-to-face courses by full classroom utilization, social distancing regulations will undoubtedly constrain the total number of residential courses that can be offered. You can only fit so many students in a classroom if the requirement is to keep everyone six feet (or more) apart. This will require that many courses be offered online, even if the students are living on (or close to) campus. How colleges and universities will build the institutional capacity to train large numbers of instructors in best practices around online course design and teaching is a difficult challenge to address, to say the least. It will depend largely on the existing instructional design and faculty development resources that are available.

Recruiting new instructional designers will likely be difficult given the high demand for these professionals right now. Some institutions may look to outsource faculty training and instructional design to online program management and other related companies. The expense of outsourcing instructional design, however, is substantial and not a guarantee of quality or faculty buy-in. This outsourcing option also may only be tenable at better-resourced institutions. Nor is it clear that outsourcing these functions is wise, as it has become increasingly clear that institutional capabilities in instructional design and online learning are core capacities in assuring institutional resilience.

The third challenge of a split curriculum model is that it does little to prepare faculty and students to pivot to a new modality should circumstances require it. If in the middle of the semester, schools are once again forced to close down campus, only a portion of the courses will be ready to shift into remote learning. The face-to-face courses could be at a disadvantage unless those courses are also designed to be hybrid courses from the beginning. While this would be prudent planning, it does create more need for already scarce design and development resources on campus.

The challenges of a split curriculum are many but perhaps no more so than many of the other scenarios schools are considering. Acknowledging that a balanced curriculum, one that emphasizes quality across all modalities, is perhaps its most important strength is a critical step if we are going to keep our students engaged. Implementing scalable training and design support to help faculty adapt their courses, learning goals, and classroom activities to an online modality is just one of the important steps worth considering.

Scenario #9

Block Plan

As practiced by institutions such as Colorado College and Cornell College, a *block plan* structures the academic semester so that students take a single course over three or four weeks. Instead of having class meetings two or three times a week, block courses might meet daily for three hours. Over the length of the semester, students take a full load of three to five courses but do so consecutively (in blocks) rather than simultaneously.

One advantage of a block plan for colleges and universities is flexibility. Moving from a traditional semester to a block schedule would allow an institution to make rapid and granular decisions if a situation requires shifting from residential to remote learning. A school could plan to have the first block in the semester consist of remote courses, with plans to move subsequent blocks to campus if the public health situation permits. Blocks also make it easier to pivot from residential back to online, should a second wave of infections occur. In conditions of uncertainty, blocks could be designed for both online and face-to-face delivery, with conditions dictating the delivery method.

Another advantage of a block plan for a university attempting to manage on-campus density is its narrow focus. The pivot to remote learning in spring 2020 because of COVID-19 has proven to be a struggle for many students. Navigating online courses requires students to practice study and time-management techniques that differ from what works for face-to-face classes. A residential semester has a structure of class meetings and deadlines, a structure to which students have become acclimated. Online learning, with its mix of asynchronous and synchronous activities, requires that students be adept at setting and sticking to study and work plans that may not be tied to specific days and times.

The challenges of developing good habits for individual study and time management for online learning are compounded by students enrolling in multiple online courses. Added to the difficulties of independently and autonomously completing the work required to manage an online course schedule, many students are also dealing with challenging home situations. However the anxiety and uncertainty of the pandemic manifest themselves in the lives of students and their families, these stressors deplete the energy and resilience students need to navigate remote learning.

A block plan might prove especially beneficial to students in a time of added stress, allowing students to narrow their focus to concentrate on succeeding in a single course. For online education, intensively participating in a single course for a relatively short time period may prove to be especially beneficial. Successful online courses are built on engagement and presence, not content or assessments. An online course community that meets frequently and exclusively will likely develop the sort of intimacy that is difficult to achieve when students' attention is spread across four or five courses. The intensity of courses in a block plan also provides space for experimentation and even failure as the depth of the learning experience will likely allow students to find opportunities to demonstrate both strengths and mastery.

For instructors, moving to a block plan will likely provide many of the same advantages of flexibility and focus enjoyed by students. By cutting the length of time that a course meets by three-quarters, but increasing the time that the course meets by a commensurate factor of four, professors can design for an intensive learning experience. This learning experience can feature elements of hands-on coaching and collaborative group work that are difficult in a normal semester-long course. Instead of sending students off to complete work independently, courses that are normally lecture- or seminar-based can be designed to mimic the experiential learning elements of lab or studio courses.

For some faculty, the prospect of spending comparatively brief but intense *sprints* with their students may be appealing. From a teaching perspective, a block plan may be particularly well-adapted to sudden shifts from residential to online learning as the still fluid and unpredictable public health situation unfolds. Pivoting a single concentrated course from residential to online, or vice versa, is likely more manageable than doing the same for a number of semester-long courses.

Considerations

Despite the evident advantages of flexibility and focus that a block plan has under conditions of a pandemic, and perhaps at any time, making the change to this course structure will likely be exceedingly difficult for most institutions. Course schedules are embedded in the larger structures of the universities in which they operate. The scheduling of courses is a mind-bogglingly complex and contingent operation, dependent on optimizing for factors as diverse as classroom utilization and student distribution requirements. Colleges and universities have evolved systems, structures, rules, and software over the years to manage the complexity of course scheduling. Moving an entire institution from a semester plan to a block plan in a matter of months is exponentially more difficult to operationalize than many suggest.

Even if the student information systems and other platforms that schools depend upon can be reprogrammed for a rapid shift to a block plan (however unlikely), it is not clear that this strategy is feasible from a time and resource perspective. Schools that operate under a block schedule have had years to refine courses and the system in which the courses are embedded. The teaching and learning culture at these schools has evolved to a point of shared expectations as well as a common understanding of the benefits and limits of block scheduling. On the other side, faculty accustomed to teaching at a comparatively leisurely pace of the full fifteen-week semester may find it very difficult to redesign their courses to fit into small, more intensive blocks. In a time of already severe disruption and discontinuity, schools may need to think hard about the wisdom of imposing any additional radical change. For every advantage of a block plan, there will be an equal and opposite consequence of this new structure, many of which are impossible to predict before the plan is in motion.

Finally, it is not immediately evident how a block plan addresses the fundamental challenge we are likely to see: the need to reduce density on campus. There may be options to mitigate this problem. One possibility, for example, is to assign some of the courses in the block as residential and others as online. Under this scenario, the block plan is layered into the split curriculum that we discussed in scenario #8. This strategy allows some students to be invited to return to campus for residential blocks, while other students participate remotely in online block courses. As with any of these decisions, how to choose which students to bring to campus and which students start the semester at home is not immediately obvious. One idea is that students could self-select between residential and online blocks. Another is that only first-year students are enrolled in the first residential block during the semester, a variant of the first-year intensive scenario we discussed in scenario #4. Each of these plans has pedagogical and student life advantages but also comes at a cost of increased complexity and the challenges inherent in any change management process. Even contemplating such wholesale changes in course scheduling, design, and delivery that the block plan demands may be unrealistic at this time.

Scenario #10

Modularity

A modular course model shares some of the features and benefits of a block plan, but with a greater degree of flexibility and variability. In essence, *modularity* considers the semester-long course structure to be one of many possible ways to organize teaching a particular topic. Some topics might lend themselves to shorter engagements, while others might be organized in such a way as to acknowledge that different students may need different sequencing. Whereas a block plan generally forces a particular structure for each course and credit unit across the entire institution (e.g., three-week modules of one course per module), a modular approach allows for much greater variation across an institution. Within a modular course model, academic departments could create courses with shorter durations and flexible start dates while keeping within the current semester structure. Unlike a block plan, which requires schools to engage in a full curricular and system redesign, shifting the course schedule from simultaneous semester-long classes to a shorter, perhaps highly integrated modular course structure could work within a traditional semester structure without too much modification.

The key to modularity is flexibility—flexible course lengths, flexible sequences, flexible topics, flexible interdependence. In a modular approach, schools, programs, departments, and even individual course sequences may all even be able to approach this flexibility differently. One option might be two 1.5-credit half-semester experiences. Another option would be to move to clusters of three-week courses that share a common, integrated week in the breaks between each cluster. Universities might define some common, agreed-upon parameters, such as the need for modules to be taught more than once a semester to give students equal opportunity to take a module regardless of their schedule. Or they might see this as an opportunity to experiment.

Modularity is an approach to curriculum design and course scheduling that has some distinct advantages during a time of public health unknowns. For students feeling disconnected from school and schoolwork because of the effects of social distancing, modular courses could help build stronger student social and learning communities. Students would be able to develop better relationships with peers across shorter, intersecting modules instead of longer classes run parallel with little intersection. Moving between highly curated modules might also help students maintain much of the initial interest and excitement that often accompanies the beginning of a new course. Anything colleges can do to help maintain connections with students is important. Additionally, modular courses that are created during and in response to the pandemic might be designed to be as topical, relevant, and immediate to students' lives as possible. Modular courses on education, wellness, public health, economic dislocations, public policy, virology, and electoral politics are just a few examples of topics that may lend themselves to this particular moment.

Modular courses that are online, short, topical, and experiential may not only relieve some pressure on campus density but may also do so in a way that is more attractive to students. Students might consider online modular experiences—ones that both contribute credit toward graduation requirements and have a different sort of rhythm and tempo than semester-long classes—as distinct from and possibly more attractive than online versions of semester-long courses. For students in residence on campus, perhaps spread across nontraditional housing options such as hotels and university-arranged long-term Airbnb rentals, participating in online modular experiences might be a particularly appealing option. Attending a semester-long online course while living in a residence hall may feel odd, but engaging in shorter, more intense, timely, and integrated online learning experiences while living on or near campus may even feel like an upgrade.

Instructors may also find short, modular course experiences an appealing departure from the traditional rhythms of teaching. The shift to a curricular structure that enables modularity could even open up the process that faculty must navigate to propose a new course, even if only temporarily. Professors could be free to experiment with new course topics and approaches. Modular online courses could move in and out of interesting problems, unique approaches, and complex curricular dynamics while also keeping students engaged in exploring *wicked* problems. Creative modular courses offer opportunities for differentiation. Faculty could create modular courses around their research specializations and use the flexible modular format to invite students into their areas of inquiry. Multiple, sequenced modular courses could be designed to serve as prerequisites to more advanced courses or for progressing through a major. Either way, faculty could be given greater license to be creative with course design and student activities.

Ultimately, the advantage of modularity is its adaptability and flexibility. Modular courses could be designed to pivot rapidly serving residential and remote students. Different learner expectations for modular courses as compared to semester-long courses could reduce friction, and ideally student and parent consternation, around online delivery. A short online modular course need not be the online analog to a residential course, it could and should be something different. As their own thing, modular courses are not burdened by history or expectations. They could be free to be new.

Considerations

The advantages that we've articulated for building modularity are intriguing, but many of these assumptions have not been tested. The idea that students may prefer short, topical, and less-formal online modules to semester-length online courses is just that, an idea. Signing up for many online modular experiences as opposed to a few semester-length online courses may in fact not prove appealing to (all) students. Part of the college experience that defines the value proposition of residential institutions is the chance to invest deeply in a topic. Students may feel that modular classes—online or face-to-face—no matter how creatively designed and relevant to their lives, are still poor substitutes for gathering around a seminar table for fifteen weeks.

Additionally, it is not immediately clear that a supply of short modular courses would actually meet the demand for reducing classroom utilization or decreasing density on campus. Short modular courses might require more space, not less. A large number of face-to-face courses might need to be taken out of the system if adequate classroom space is to be freed up for smaller modular courses. Any plan that contemplates modularity as the answer to the puzzle of dedensification should first confirm that there is enough classroom space to handle core courses under conditions of social distancing, even with most electives removed from these spaces.

Modularity may also be particularly challenging for faculty, whose capacity is severely stretched. Faculty may be excited to offer a single new concise, topical, and experiential online learning experience, but designing these modules is no easy feat. Similarly, while it may be possible to design modules that sequence together to meet course prerequisites or the requirements of a major, this would take a good deal of planning. Some majors are highly prescriptive, with students having to fill their course schedules with required courses and only infrequently enjoying the option of signing up for an elective. For professors teaching both full-term residential (or possibly online) courses and modular courses, it may be particularly difficult to design courses and modules on different schedules. Relatedly, how modular courses factor into faculty load becomes a complex problem in and of itself. This may be solvable but the solution might require complex internal institutional negotiations that might be more than any school could bear right now.

Whichever way a school chooses to introduce some elements of modularity as a strategy, it is highly likely that the long-run results of this approach could prove generative in the evolution of the curriculum. The freedom for professors to create and teach short, topical, and experiential courses would enrich and enliven the campus learning ecosystem long after the pandemic has passed. For students, modular courses that speak closely to their concerns and their challenges, and which are a break from the regular rhythms of the full semester (or quarter) may prove to be restorative and invigorating. A silver lining of COVID-19 could end up being an accelerated pace of curricular innovation, with modularity a prime example of this sort of progress.

Scenario #11

Students in Residence Learning Virtually

In the scenario where there are *students in residence learning virtually*, residential colleges and universities would teach courses online while students live together on campus. Prior to COVID-19, this approach was most directly associated with the Minerva Schools at KGI (Keck Graduate Institute). This partnership between the for-profit Minerva Project and the nonprofit Keck Graduate Institute integrates an in-residence learning experience (in multiple global cities) with courses delivered through an online platform. The Minerva Schools at KGI example is instructive in thinking about a students in residence learning virtually scenario. Part of the argument of the Minerva experiment (or business model) is that online courses have the potential to offer traditional college-age undergraduates a superior learning experience to face-to-face classes.

What online learning does less well, the argument goes, is to provide students an immersive and experiential educational environment. Those experiences—the socializing and playing and networking, the team projects and late-night discussions—happen best when students are physically together. They can't be easily replicated online. Minerva solves this problem by bringing students together in common living situations while still holding classes online. They live in the same building, eat together, socialize all in person. When classes start, they return to their rooms to get online to learn together in a virtual environment.

In the scenario of students in residence learning virtually, colleges and universities attempt to preserve much of this social engagement in on-campus living while also maximizing flexibility around the fluid public health situation by teaching all courses online. Despite potentially seeming counterintuitive, this approach has some significant advantages. Perhaps first and foremost is that this would allow campuses to make flexible, adaptive decisions about students in residence based on the constantly changing public health information. If the public health situation warrants, (some or all) students could be asked to return home while instruction would simply continue as it had been. This approach also would allow for a relatively dynamic quarantining of students who test positive for the disease. Assuming they are not showing symptoms, they could continue classes relatively easily since the courses would all be online.

Having students living on campus would also allow for targeted use of campus resources, such as the library, labs, internet access, and technology support. Students in the greatest need of campus support services such as academic resource centers and student health and counseling services could have access on campus while observing social distancing guidelines. Depending on the size and technology of classrooms at a given school, keeping all the instruction online would allow schools to avoid potentially expensive investments in classroom upgrades for blended courses or to design complex course schedules to take advantage of the larger classrooms on campus, classrooms that would be necessary even for small enrollment courses to maintain social distancing.

Colleges and universities have experience now teaching online. Throughout the strictest periods of stay-at-home orders at the initial height of pandemic's virulence, colleges and universities remained open for business by moving courses to a remote learning environment. Classes were taught, papers were submitted, exams were taken, and credit was conferred. Having students in residence learning virtually maintains the online learning experience while layering in a residential experience as public health restrictions are loosened, assuming of course that some social distancing guidelines will be flexible enough to allow for residence on campus but restrictive enough to warrant continued remote learning.

Considerations

One challenge of the students in residence learning virtually scenario is that faculty would be asked to plan to teach online. Despite what we said earlier, teaching online is still a relatively new experience for most faculty. Good course designs for online and residential learning experiences share many common elements: Backward course design. Aligning student activities with learning objectives. An emphasis on formative rather than summative assessment. And a prioritization of presence, care, and community. Despite these core similarities, online and residential courses require different and distinct strategies to succeed. Colleges and universities would need to work with faculty to help them adapt from one mode to another. Students would be on campus and would expect high-quality online courses. All faculty, from tenured to contingent, would need to be given the time, resources, and support to make this happen, just as the school would need to recognize the extensive time and energy required to do so. That recognition might come in the form of future course releases, lower caps on course enrollments, and a positive impact on annual reviews and in the promotion and tenure process.

Another challenge of students in residence learning virtually is an effect of one of its greatest strengths. While a distinct virtue of this approach is its inherent flexibility—students could move off campus quickly without disrupting academic progress—this kind of pivot will still hit students with the greatest need of support (via internet access, stable living environment, funding and resources, accessibility and accommodation) the hardest. A flexible approach might mean schools would unintentionally pay less attention to helping students be prepared for the potential pivot if it were to come. It would be important for schools not only to prepare for the online mode but to help their students prepare for a potential move back home.

The third challenge of this scenario is its impact on international students. Students from outside the United States make up a significant percentage of students at an increasingly broad number of institutions. These students are perhaps least likely to be able to return to campus. Developing an educational strategy that assumes that students will be in residence and learning virtually could pose significant problems for international students if they are not considered in the design process.

A fourth challenge has to do with housing. As we have highlighted throughout our tour of scenarios, maintaining social distancing while providing a bundled campus-based education may be both academic and residential, but the residential piece may prove to be the most difficult to address. Figuring out how to spread beds and bathrooms apart is significantly more difficult than creating scenarios for social distance in classrooms. The definition of the residence hall is likely to expand to encompass campus-adjacent hotels and long-term rentals of private homes. But these choices may not be possible at many schools, and the idea of creating a socially distant residential space on a residential campus may exacerbate inequities and accessibility issues.

In the final analysis, students in residence learning virtually depends on the ability of campuses to absorb a critical mass of campus-housed students. Developing educational plans under the assumption that most students will be living on or near campus will drive different course designs and teaching strategies than planning for students to learn online from their homes. This could lead to many exciting and dynamic learning experiences while still offering students at residential schools rich, on-campus college experiences.

Scenario #12

Low-Residency

A *low-residency* model builds on the experience of numerous colleges and universities that offer online master's programs with significant residential components. Courses in a low-residency model include both online and face-to-face components. The face-to-face part typically occurs in short bursts of intense daylong sessions that run for a weekend or a week. For the rest of the time, students live and learn at home online.

The on-campus time in a low-residency course takes advantage of the compressed time students are on campus to create highly focused face-to-face sessions designed to build community, launch group projects, and introduce complex topics in highly responsive, often discussion-based activities. Lectures and labs might be a part of the on-campus experience, but these traditional face-to-face elements are augmented by experiential activities with a focus on social learning. Because of this immersive approach, a large portion of a course's contact hours is highly concentrated when students are on campus, though the majority of them still occur online. If a typical course has 45–48 contact hours, a third of those might be accounted for during the residential period.

Traditionally, low-residency graduate programs endeavor to provide adult, working participants the flexibility of online learning while also providing the immersive and social learning advantages that are possible through campus-based face-to-face experiences. Translating a low-residency approach would require adapting this model to work across a much larger number of students, perhaps even the entire campus. Adopting a low-residency model for all students would potentially enable a high proportion of learners to have a campus experience, albeit one that is relatively brief. The advantage of building the term or semester around a low-residency model is that students will still receive the sort of social, experiential, and intensive residential experience that defines much of the perceived value of attending a residential institution. The difference is that these experiences are highly concentrated over a short period of time, rather than a full term or semester.

The length of the residential experience in a low-residency model could depend on a number of factors. One factor, for example, could be a calculation of how many students a campus can safely accommodate under conditions of social distancing. In this approach, the fewer students that can be safely housed in residence halls and taught in classrooms, the more the student body must be divided into discrete residential groups. For example, if a school decides it could safely accommodate one-quarter of all its students at any given time, it could design a robust low-residency model based on this number. The school could divide the student body into four segments that can safely be on campus at one time. From there a school might decide it wants to bring students to campus for extended blocks (three weeks, say, to allow for all students to rotate through campus) or short bursts (as short as a weekend). While the block schedule is similar to the block plan we described in scenario #9, a low-residency approach has blocks supplemented by off-campus, online learning built into the design.

On the other hand, a short-burst approach instead of a low-residency block plan would enable schools to be more flexible, potentially allowing them to bring students back to campus for multiple visits. Students could come one weekend in the first month, depending on the scalability of on-campus housing because of social distance guidelines, and then return at the midpoint to present a midterm project. A final visit to campus might allow students to wrap up final projects in person.

Alternative constructions for managing a low-residency model can be easily imagined, of course. Each will come with strengths and weaknesses. For example, courses could be categorized by residential periods based on class-size dynamics, course content, or a whole host of possible configurations. In this approach, each category would correspond to a set date range. Students would then be able to enroll only in courses designated for residency within a designated range. If a semester contained four residencies

(A, B, C, and D), then students would only register for courses with a single residency identifier.

These ideas are meant to illuminate the concept rather than suggest a set of complete solutions. Building the academic experience around a low-residency model offers numerous opportunities to mix, match, and blend many of the fifteen scenarios we have been discussing, as well to integrate many that we have not mentioned. Combining online courses with intense residential periods to achieve acceptable levels of campus density, while maximizing the proportion of students who receive some residential experience, will likely be compelling to many universities. The strategy builds on a known and successful methodology (low-residency graduate programs) while addressing some of the concerns about academic continuity and the desire for a residential experience under COVID-19.

Considerations

Implementing a low-residency model at an institutional scale will likely prove significantly (if not exponentially) more challenging than the other scenarios we have been discussing. The first difficulties come in scheduling and logistics. Creating a course plan that merges online and in-person classes for every course and every student is likely beyond the capabilities of the existing scheduling and course management infrastructure. Logistically, it is not clear that campuses could handle the multiple move-in/move-out days that bringing most students briefly to campus would require. The requirement to clean residence halls and ready them for each successive wave of students may also be beyond even the most robust capabilities of facilities and residential life.

From a faculty point of view, the time necessary to design an online course integrated with an intensive residential experience would be substantial. Even if nine-month faculty contracts were not a factor, it is unclear that professors would have enough time or institutional support to develop rich low-residency courses. This educational model would also put large demands on the campus professionals who have been working with instructors during the emergency transition to remote learning and who collaborate with professors during more normal times. Quality low-residency courses at the graduate school level are often designed and run by a team of faculty and nonfaculty educators. Contributors include librarians, learning designers, and educational technologists, among many others. The number of people occupying those roles on campus has not increased during the pandemic, and they are already spread thin.

From an access and equity standpoint, a low-residency model requires students to both absorb travel costs for the brief campus stays while managing the challenges inherent in online learning. Students living in homes with fast internet connections and quiet places to study enjoy significant educational advantages compared to their classmates with neither. As we've been saying, this is a problem inherent in many approaches, and we think it important for schools to keep this issue front and center. Our students need outreach, support, and engagement to help them understand how best to learn in the current environment. Implementing a low-residency model would come with new challenges for our students for which schools would need to be prepared.

Finally, from an institutional perspective, a low-residency model comes with numerous challenges beyond scheduling and logistics. Courses with campus-based requirements are unlikely to be accessible to international students. Any student who is unable to travel to campus for a low-residency period, for whatever reason, would miss out on the educational opportunities that campus-intensive interactions can offer. Students used to a class schedule made up of hour-long to ninety-minute blocks would need to learn how to be effective in intense, daylong sessions.

For these reasons and others, it's difficult to imagine many (if any) schools adopting this model. The model does, however, serve a role in the preparation, design, and thinking all schools are undertaking right now. They might ask, if we are fully remote is there some advantage to imagining scaled low-residency for some students? If we are fully remote, could the intense engagements of low-residency be played out in local communities of students that many schools have across the country and the world? If we are fully remote, could we imagine a low-residency structure for the end of the semester rather than the beginning? These and other similar questions could help a school be more creative, more thoughtful, and more focused as it considers its options designing the low-density university.

Scenario #13

HyFlex

If there is one scenario that may be adopted more than others, it could well be the *HyFlex* model.[14] This may be because a hybrid, or "high flexibility," approach is relatively easy to envision. In HyFlex, a term first coined by Brian Beatty, courses are delivered both in person and online at the same time by the same faculty member. Students can then choose for each and every class meeting whether to show up for the class in person or to join it online. The underlying design ethos behind the HyFlex model is flexibility and student choice.

For HyFlex to work, the classroom needs to be set up with, at minimum, a camera, video conferencing capabilities, and some way of interacting with the students at a distance. Classes are streamed live and could be recorded for later playback. Professors interact with both in-person and online synchronous learners, through platforms such as Zoom or Teams. Class recordings might be complemented by asynchronous discussion boards and other collaborative tools in the campus learning management system. Advanced HyFlex classroom set-ups might include such technology as monitors around the edges of the classroom space that allow professors to see and address students who are participating live in the class at a distance. Perhaps the zenith of HyFlex is the RealPresence Experience rooms that

14. "7 Things You Should Know about the HyFlex Course Model," EDUCAUSE Learning Initiative (ELI), updated July 7, 2020, https://library.educause.edu/resources/2010/11/7-things-you-should-know-about-the-hyflex-course-model.

some schools have installed, with students at a distance all appearing life-sized on a large screen in a specially designed classroom.

The appeal to some of the HyFlex model is its flexibility. Courses could be placed in a regular campus classroom schedule. As social distancing requirements shift, the number of students in the face-to-face classroom environment can expand. Students who are unable to attend the in-class sessions can fully participate online, either synchronously or, in some cases, asynchronously. HyFlex, at least in its original conception, is designed for students who live on or close by to campus. It was not meant as a solution for distance education. Instead, it was meant to give residential and commuter students the flexibility to attend class in person or remotely. This flexibility is attractive when the effects of the pandemic are forcing schools to make decisions about how many students can fit into a classroom on campus, even if they live on or near campus. The conceptual flexibility of this model also enables it to function for students who may not be able to attend class on campus at all, which might be the case for some international students unable to return to the United States even if domestic students are able to live on campus.

For students, a HyFlex model holds the potential of maximizing the opportunity to participate in a face-to-face learning experience under conditions of social distancing. How this is managed might vary from school to school. A professor might divide her class up into groups, with each group switching (or rotating, if there are more than two groups) between face-to-face and online instruction. Students might be given the opportunity to sign up for residential learning slots for each class session, up until the "safe" number of in-person spaces is taken. Or in-class slots could be assigned randomly or prioritized along dimensions of student need. Or perhaps, more importantly, students who test positive for COVID-19 and need to quarantine could attend class remotely while they are not showing symptoms. It's important to note that the goal of HyFlex is to make both the online and in-person experiences equal. Participation in class is necessary regardless of where and how students attend. Online is not meant to be a diminished experience but an alternative. Class sessions are not meant to be passive observations of a class video stream, but rather to have fully interactive engagements, including Q&A, group work (if possible), and student presentations.

For schools, the HyFlex model offers the potential to resume face-to-face teaching, despite uncertainties about the number of students that campus classrooms can safely accommodate. Class lectures could be delivered to a classroom of at least some students, enabling the sort of real-time student reactions and interactions on which professors appreciate (and which they often find harder to recreate in an online environment). Another advantage for faculty is that the structure of a HyFlex does not only have to involve students attending online. Faculty could be the ones who are remote (or shift between face-to-face and remote teaching as public health and personal circumstances change). They could teach from home to a classroom of in-person students and a group of online students at the same time. For faculty concerned about their health and safety, teaching at a distance would give them flexibility, while still giving students the opportunity to work together (albeit in a socially distanced manner).

In discussions with colleagues in leadership roles across the postsecondary ecosystem, the HyFlex model is mentioned often. In an environment of both a strong (almost existential) desire to resume residential educational operations, combined with an almost total lack of certainty around what the public health situation will look like, a HyFlex approach holds out the promise of resuming classroom teaching and learning, while also being flexible enough to accommodate the full range of synchronous and asynchronous online learning modalities.

Considerations

It might sound as if HyFlex is the perfect solution. Social distancing? Check. On-campus instruction? Check. Online flexibility? Check. But, navigating the challenges of teaching to both in-person and online students, while also creating rich interactive learning experiences for students participating in the course asynchronously, is hard. If done poorly, faculty run the risk of making the students at a distance feel like second-class citizens. The last thing anyone who advocates for a HyFlex approach would want is for online students to find themselves "watching" rather than fully participating in class. Without careful thought and intentional design, online students are likely to be at a distinct disadvantage in faculty attention and learning opportunities.

To do it well, then, a lot of things need to line up, including the technology, the course design, the focus on pedagogy, and the engagement of the students. Many schools that wish to scale the HyFlex model across the curriculum will likely need to make a significant investment in classroom technology. Since intentionally designed rooms with sophisticated cameras, microphones, and monitors are the foundation of any good HyFlex classroom, the choice to adopt this approach may come down to cost. For many schools, it might be too expensive to outfit fully the needed number of classrooms over the summer, while not doing so runs the risk of creating more barriers than points of entry for their students. Making the wrong investment can be just as bad. While cameras are important, perhaps the most crucial pieces of equipment are quality microphones to pick up sounds in the room. Without good microphones, the students online are at a distinct disadvantage.

While most concerns about the HyFlex model tend to focus on the not insubstantial technological requirements for running a mixed modality course, the person requirements of this method are no less important. To take full advantage of the technology and the focus on teaching, faculty need help. The most sophisticated tracking cameras and multipoint microphone arrays will not alone overcome the difficulty of juggling both the in-class and live online students. The largest institutional investments at many schools may in fact be in teams of people. Teams who help train faculty and serve as learning designers and classroom technology professionals collaborating with faculty on designing and running a HyFlex course.

Finally, the best HyFlex classrooms have someone assisting the faculty member. These assistants are often called upon to take an active role in the in-class sessions, helping the instructor incorporate questions and feedback from remote learners in real time. In some cases, media professionals participate in the class session to capture both faculty and students for the streamed and recorded versions of the class session. These assistants could also be work-study students who are assigned a particular classroom (or digital space), or they might be volunteers from class who are given credit for assisting in the delivery of the course.

It's this last role that we think worth reinforcing. So much of what we have been talking about in this scenario (and across all fifteen scenarios) is how schools are thinking about academic continuity and how faculty will need to prepare to teach in these flexible environments. But one of the most important things for schools to consider is how students are asked to participate in their learning. We often assume that these scenarios are just about preparing for the students as if the students are just consumers.

This new normal of teaching and learning needs to be different than it was when schools shifted to emergency remote learning in the spring of 2020. We need to ask students to be part of the solution of allowing learning to flourish. This includes asking them to help manage the class if it has a virtual component. It means asking students to work with us as we prepare and teach. It means asking them to serve as in-class course assistants and technology guides. It means making this help part of the course grade and part of their experience.

Perhaps most important, whatever scenario a campus chooses, it must include outreach to students now and going forward. Students need to see that they are part of the campus community and they need to be engaged in this difficult work. This is incredibly important if a HyFlex model is to be successful, and it's even more important (and perhaps valuable) in the next discussion of a modified tutorial model.

Scenario #14

Modified Tutorial

The *modified tutorial* model leans heavily on students as partners. In some versions of the tutorial approach, students might take a common lecture and then meet with the faculty member or teaching assistant in small recitations. In others, they might only meet one-on-one or in very small groups to do the work of the course. In a modified tutorial model, the common lecture could be delivered online and the small meetings could be structured to follow social distancing requirements. The goal of any tutorial model, modified or otherwise, is to develop deep, meaningful, and perhaps even personalized learning experiences.

Arguably this model is as old as formal teaching (and perhaps older, since it is in some respects the collegiate equivalent of the apprenticeship model, or what is often referred to as cognitive or intellectual apprenticeship). To this day, Oxford University and others still employ versions of this one-on-one type of tutorial, while University of Cambridge's supervisions model has a similar approach but in smaller groups.[15] Most schools likely have something akin to these kinds of tutorials. Many schools have small specialized programs, such as honors programs, in which a faculty member works one-on-one with a student on a thesis. The lecture/recitation

15. "How Will I Be Taught?," University of Cambridge, Undergraduate Study, accessed May 30, 2020, https://www.undergraduate.study.cam.ac.uk/courses/how-will-i-be-taught.

structure attempts, in part, a scaled version of this kind of tutorial, albeit with the demands of a large student body in mind.

For colleges and universities attempting to reduce density while still looking to implement a high-touch teaching and learning experience, a modified tutorial model could be a very attractive approach. Like many of the scenarios we have been discussing, a modified tutorial model has many possible variations, and how it might be implemented could come down to a number of factors, from cost to concerns about faculty time to the availability of tutors or TAs. Many approaches to this model, though, could take advantage of both the affordances of available technology and the need for social distancing.

How might a modified tutorial model work? One approach would be to flip the classroom. Lectures or didactic material could be delivered online asynchronously. Faculty or teaching assistants could then meet with their students in small groups. The smaller the groups, the better the experience would likely be for the students. Another approach, perhaps for smaller, discussion-based classes, would be to run the entire class as a small tutorial. Instead of one eighteen-person class meeting three times a week, the faculty member might meet in small groups of say six students once a week. Or perhaps even more often for shorter periods of time. The goal would not be to divide the scheduled in-class time into equal parts based on the number of small groups but instead to rethink the class time to encourage deeper engagement and more meaningful community building. These concerns are even more crucial given social distancing requirements to wear masks and to stand behind plexiglass in standard classrooms.

In this approach, faculty might have to spend more time in smaller group meetings, but they would have richer engagements with their students. They could also possibly eliminate time spent on other activities. Or, if this approach is combined with a targeted curriculum or block plan, faculty whose courses were suspended or who are not teaching during a particular block could take on the role of running tutorials with students. This time could also be distributed to TAs or even alumni who might be asked to participate. A modified tutorial model could be an excellent way to involve recent graduates passionate about their alma mater who would like to help during a time when schools are facing unprecedented challenges. Either of these could save faculty members significant amounts of time they could devote to creating course materials or working with students in greatest need.

Perhaps a more engaging approach, though, would be to involve students in the courses in facilitating tutorial sessions. Students could be asked to prepare discussion prompts, meet with their peers, and participate in class in new and dynamic ways. Students running a tutorial in any given week might have an extended discussion session with the faculty member to help them prepare. As almost any faculty member will acknowledge, we tend to learn more about something when we have to teach it. A modified tutorial model lends itself to project-based learning extremely well, where students could be asked to take on different roles as projects evolve. For students, a modified tutorial could lead to a richer, deeper learning experience where they are asked to engage with the material not just as passive consumers but as active intellectual apprentices. Students serving as peer tutors and those participating in class would have smaller, more intimate learning experiences at a time when this personal interaction will be too easily lost.

Besides a deep investment in personalized learning, another advantage of a modified tutorial model is its potential flexibility. Tutorials could be held on campus, in person in small socially distant groups, or online, perhaps rotating between locations as the semester continues. Tutorials could also allow for a quick pivot online or off campus as the health situation requires. Faculty concerned about their health and safety could meet with groups at a distance, while TAs or peer tutors could meet on campus with students. The flexibility of this model may make it particularly appealing to university leaders who must draw up plans in which the public health situation remains unknown. Efforts during the summer could be focused on the development of the asynchronous online portions of courses, with the decision to hold small tutorial meetings face-to-face or online made when the feasibility of bringing students back to campus becomes more clear.

Considerations

The goal of a modified tutorial model is to develop deep, meaningful, and perhaps even personalized learning experiences with as much flexibility as possible. The challenges, while smaller than some of the models we have been exploring, are worth considering. The biggest may be time and resources. There are limits, for example, to the number of small groups of students that a professor can engage in discussion, conversation, and debate. Breaking a class of twenty or thirty into small tutorial groups for synchronous online or face-to-face discussions with a professor may be manageable, if logistically challenging. Expecting that a professor alone can run tutorial sessions for small groups drawn from a large-enrollment course, however, is difficult to envision. Any consideration of a modified tutorial model would need to be made against the availability and willingness of faculty to embrace this different expectation on their time inherent in this approach.

A challenge, then, for any implementation of a modified tutorial model is mitigating the potential for increased demands on faculty time. As student participation and discussion are channeled into small group meetings in at least one version of this model, the content delivery aspects of a course might be concentrated in asynchronous online materials. This likely involves the recording of lectures, the development of formative and summative online assessments, and perhaps the deployment of online simulations and interactive exercises.

These online elements are input-intensive. Creating quality, concise recorded lectures, or breaking up longer lectures into smaller more digestible chunks appropriate for online learning, requires faculty to invest additional time and effort. While a newly hired and trained army of teaching and learning assistants can certainly help, professors will likely still need to spend time creating the content and assessments of the online asynchronous course. A modified tutorial model might help reduce density in the classroom by moving the least socially distant element of a course—the lecture delivered in a lecture hall—to online recorded lectures, exercises, and assessments. This reduction in classroom density, however, might come at the price of faculty time to develop online course materials.

Perhaps the bigger expense of faculty time, though, is the potential time meeting with students. If schools are unable to hire TAs or adopt curricula in which students in a class serve as peer tutors, faculty may be asked to spend more time meeting with students than they are used to. This increased expectation of time is difficult to ask at any school, especially when faculty are spread thin trying to manage teaching in a new, socially distanced mode. Any successful implementation of a modified tutorial model will likely need to employ teaching assistants and peer tutors. Involving students in their learning as course assistants has benefits beyond those of reducing the amount of time a faculty member can devote to any one course. Faculty will be asked to adopt teaching approaches that they are unfamiliar with. Students will be asked to learn in new modes and ways of being on and off campus.

The best thing any school can do is to bring students into the teaching and learning process. Asking students to serve as course assistants—as learning assistants—helps deepen their experience with the course material, but more than this it helps students see they are part of a learning community. They are part of a body of people creating and exchanging knowledge. And perhaps most importantly, they can contribute to this activity.

Scenario #15

Fully Remote

Our final scenario, *fully remote*, envisions a situation where the public health situation will not allow students, faculty, or staff to return to campus. Students would learn and faculty would continue to teach from wherever they are. Campuses would remain open only with skeletal staffing levels. Cocurricular activities, to the extent possible, would be virtualized. In many respects, this scenario—along with the first scenario of going back to normal—is the most straightforward. It is, however, not without its challenges.

The greatest challenge is, perhaps, an issue of perception. Many faculty and students do not consider online education to be equivalent to face-to-face classes,[16] despite substantial evidence that online learning can be as effective or more so than face-to-face learning.[17] This perception was reinforced by the hasty move to remote learning in spring 2020, and residential colleges and universities are highly reluctant to signal they are considering a fully remote scenario. Quite the opposite. Mitch Daniels, the president of Purdue, made headlines when he announced that Purdue intended to enroll

16. Carrie Anne Platt, Amber N. W. Raile, and Nan Yu, "Virtually the Same?: Student Perceptions of the Equivalence of Online Classes to Face-to-Face Classes," *MERLOT Journal of Online Learning and Teaching* 10, no. 3 (December 2014): 489–503, https://jolt.merlot.org/vol10no3/Platt_0914.pdf.

17. Tuan Nguyen, "The Effectiveness of Online Learning: Beyond No Significant Difference and Future Horizons," *MERLOT Journal of Online Learning and Teaching* 11, no. 2 (June 2015): 309–19, https://jolt.merlot.org/Vol11no2/Nguyen_0615.pdf.

students "on campus in typical numbers this fall."[18] Christina Paxson, the president of Brown University, argued similarly for the need to be back on campus in a *New York Times* opinion piece entitled "College Campuses Must Reopen in the Fall. Here's How We Do It."[19]

Despite the full-throated and public commitments by university leaders that fully remote is not on the table, it's difficult for any school to dismiss the possibility completely, especially considering that institutions may have little choice in the matter. With nationwide spikes in infections and hospitalizations beyond what local ICU's can handle, schools may have no option but to continue with remote learning. Similarly, if accurate rapid testing kits remain unavailable in the numbers needed, schools may be unable to monitor the health and enact appropriate quarantine measures of residential students.

Is it possible for colleges and universities to be fully remote due to public health necessity, while offering their students an educational experience commensurate with a residential semester? From a purely teaching and learning perspective, fully remote might be preferable for some schools over many of the mixed residential and online scenarios that we have been discussing. One challenge of mixing residential and remote students for many institutions is providing a level playing field for all learners. Dividing the attention of faculty in course design and teaching between face-to-face and online modalities could potentially dilute the quality of both, particularly at schools without resources to support faculty as they invest in this work. Approaches such as the modified tutorial model seek to overcome these challenges in hybrid learning by bringing students into the teaching and learning process, but it poses its own challenges in terms of faculty bandwidth and the need for institutions to see their students as participants in their learning rather than consumers of it.

On the other hand, going fully remote might give faculty the opportunity to build on their experiences with what worked and what did not in the design and delivery of their remote classes. If decisions were made early

18. Purdue University, "A Message from President Daniels regarding Fall Semester," accessed April 21, 2020, https://www.purdue.edu/president/messages/campus-community/2020/2004-fall-message.php.

19. Christina Paxson, "College Campuses Must Reopen in the Fall. Here's How We Do It," *New York Times*, April 26, 2020, https://www.nytimes.com/2020/04/26/opinion/coronavirus-colleges-universities.html.

enough, schools will have had months instead of days to build training and support structures to help professors think about the best possible ways to design and teach courses in a fully remote environment. Online student support services and cocurricular activities could potentially be strengthened. Colleges and universities will have some space and time (albeit limited) to make the transition from "emergency remote instruction" to full "online learning." To do so well would mean the adoption of a set of course design practices and pedagogical strategies that have demonstrated long-term empirical success in producing quality learning outcomes in online courses and programs. The variation in course design quality and the student learning experience that was present in remote courses could begin to smooth out if schools invest in this approach.

Considerations

The overwhelming resistance by many schools to consider going fully remote is, perhaps, driven as much by financial necessity as by educational concerns, despite existing biases against online learning. The loss of revenues for fixed expenses such as residence halls and other campus services has been devastating to the balance sheets of colleges and universities. A significant loss of tuition dollars if students choose to forgo enrollment out of concerns about the value remote learning represents could be an existential risk for some institutions, and a deeply difficult financial challenge for all.

These obstacles for a fully remote approach were attenuated, to some extent, during the spring of 2020. As every residential college and university made the emergency shift from campus-based to virtual classes in the spring, students and their parents were (for the most part) flexible and mostly understanding. While there were some calls for refunds, demands for schools to give back (or dramatically lower) tuition for remote courses were largely muted.[20] It's unclear if this goodwill will continue if colleges and universities believe it is necessary to maintain a fully remote posture to protect the health of students, faculty, and staff—as well as the communities in which campuses are embedded. The continuation of remote learning

20. Greta Anderson, "Feeling Shortchanged," *Inside Higher Ed*, April 13, 2020, https://www.insidehighered.com/news/2020/04/13/students-say-online-classes-arent-what-they-paid.

may push some proportion of students to turn the 2020–2021 academic year into a gap year. Still other students may continue their studies but choose to enroll in online courses at a less expensive community college, assuming (perhaps incorrectly) that they would be able to transfer the earned credits when campuses return to on-campus education.

To face this challenge of student melt, schools are working hard to make their remote learning plans as rich and dynamic as possible. Shifting from emergency remote teaching to an ongoing fully remote instructional strategy could allow faculty to focus both their energies and attention. The range of support structures that enable and assist students and professors in their learning could be optimized for virtual learners. The institutional focus of attention, energy, and resources that would be difficult to achieve in a mixed online/remote structure might be possible if faculty were focused on teaching fully online.

It will be expensive, however, for universities to continue in a fully remote mode. These expenses would come at a time of considerable financial challenges, driven by both rising costs and uncertainty about students' willingness to continue to pay full tuition costs. While it is true that online learning can be as effective as face-to-face learning, it often takes extensive resources and hard work to make robust online courses. The few months we have to make going fully remote a success are one-third (or less) of the time fully online courses typically take to develop. And this is with a full team of learning designers, media specialists, and faculty developers working with one faculty member. To teach an online course well is often substantially more work for faculty. Asking more of our faculty at a time when everyone is already stretched thin may be difficult.

Despite this, the decision to remain fully remote may be palatable to institutions with limited residential learners. Institutions with mostly commuter students may feel greater flexibility in delaying the restart of classroom-based courses. On the other hand, community colleges, with missions built around expanded access and equity, are likely to have significant concerns about the ability of all their students to thrive in a remote learning environment. These schools may need to consider how to support online students with resources like success coaching and the availability of loaner laptops. This, too, is expensive, especially for our schools that have had their public funding continually reduced.

No matter how we look at it, the ability of institutions of higher learning to continue to serve as engines of opportunity, as well as the sources of societal knowledge creation, depends on the ability of schools to balance the books. The combination of eroding public support, demographic headwinds, and the necessity of tuition discounting to fill classes has left most of the sector in a precarious economic situation before the pandemic. Federal financial support from the CARES Act, while welcome, provides nowhere near the level of funds to match the additional expenses that schools have absorbed during the pandemic and will be completely inadequate should revenues drop precipitously.[21] Separating economic concerns from educational if schools must remain fully remote is difficult. The education of students is inextricably intertwined with how that education is paid for. The longer colleges and universities are unable to resume residential student operations and face-to-face classes, the more difficult the financial situation of schools will become.

21. Madeline St. Amour, "Federal Funding Left Out Some of the Most Vulnerable," *Inside Higher Ed*, April 23, 2020, https://www.insidehighered.com/news/2020/04/23/community-colleges-regional-publics-lost-formula-cares-act-funds.

II. EQUITY, PLACE, AND LEARNING

Until an effective vaccine for COVID-19 is developed and widely distributed, the reality is that the future of residential education is uncertain. At the time of this writing, some schools have announced plans, while others are still in the planning stages. Some of the announced plans were covered in our discussions of the scenarios (*Fully Remote*, *HyFlex*, *Students in Residence Learning Virtually*) and others were ones we mentioned but didn't discuss fully (*Late Start*). The point of our developing these scenarios was never to provide an exhaustive or exclusive list of strategies for universities during this unprecedented time. Our goal, instead, was to provide our colleagues with a framework in which planning can occur. A good framework provides both a structure in which decisions can be evaluated as well as a set of defined terms that can help ensure a baseline of shared understanding.

The overnight shift from residential to remote learning in spring 2020 revealed much about what matters most, and what accounts for little, in the bundle of services, structures, and relationships that constitute higher education. As the 2020–2021 academic year unfolds, we will learn more. At this point in the story of higher education under threat of COVID-19, at least three themes have come into focus: equity, place, and learning.

Equity

The first area that the system-wide pivot to remote learning illuminates has to do with equity. What we are learning during the pandemic is that residential education can act (if imperfectly and unevenly) to normalize at least some aspects of the college experience. While it remains very much the case that success in college is not randomly distributed, with students from more privileged backgrounds retaining many advantages across measures of student success (attrition, STEM success, time to graduation, etc.), it is also true that residential education does create some opportunity for success that may not be available to all students in their home lives. Students from less privileged backgrounds might not come to campus with the advantages of years of tutoring or access to resources from well-funded secondary schools, but the experience of being an undergraduate offers some consistency of opportunity that may not necessarily be available to all students at home. First-year students from different backgrounds have access to space in residence halls. Students from across the socioeconomic spectrum attend class in the same classrooms, study in the same library, and work out in the same athletic center. Wealthier students may have newer computers than their less well-off peers, but everyone logs into the same Wi-Fi.

Again, we don't wish to deny or minimize that there are huge differences in opportunity faced by students within any given college or university based on their backgrounds and access to resources. Too many of our students must navigate the basic challenges of housing, food, and educational materials—even within wealthy universities. Students of color and LGBTQ students continue to face significant issues of bias and harm on campuses across the country. First-generation students are often at a disadvantage in managing the expectations of college. These issues can make it incredibly difficult to be a successful college student. Many residential campuses acknowledge this and try to do better. They have developed support structures to address some of these disparities and work toward equality of opportunity.

The pandemic has both revealed and exacerbated the higher education opportunity divide. We've seen just how important access to these fundamental services and these basic support structures are to the well-being and success of many of our students. During the months of enforced remote learning, we have witnessed how advantages in resources can accrue into advantages in learning. Students with private places to study, reliable Wi-Fi, and less economically stressed home environments enjoy tangible benefits in their efforts to navigate online courses. If the future of higher education might include less time spent on campus, then colleges and universities will need to figure out how to extend the residential-based resources that students rely on for success to a more virtualized environment.

During the initial response to the spread of the novel coronavirus, the role of supporting learners through complicated and difficult situations often fell to faculty and staff. Since then, professors and support staff have been on the front lines of responding to the broad array of student needs. Going forward, and even if we return to a situation that resembles prepandemic higher education, it is likely that faculty and staff will have a sharpened appreciation and knowledge of the obstacles and challenges that their students face. How this knowledge will impact pedagogy as well as the institutional structures designed to bolster student success are questions that should be top of mind for everyone who works in higher education.

As schools think about the teaching and learning under requirements of reduced campus density and social distancing, student success will depend heavily on their access to the fundamental services of their institutions. Without careful attention, moving away from residential education will likely result in *less* equity, particularly in areas of student learning and other student success outcomes. Each of the scenarios we proposed in this book impacts this access in different ways. Decisions around timing—when the semester starts—could keep students away from these services longer. Choices about student population and location might disadvantage certain students over others. This is especially true if the scenarios are taken as sacrosanct. We expect and hope that all schools are in fact adjusting these scenarios based on the unique characteristics of their student body and institutional circumstances as they work to support their students in greatest need.

Place

A second theme that emerges in thinking about the coming academic year through the lens of *15 Scenarios* is an evolving understanding of place. While only three of the scenarios are explicitly about location (*Students in Residence Learning Virtually*, *Low-Residency*, and *HyFlex*), the industry-wide rapid pivot from residential to remote learning has revealed some new things about the idea of place in higher education. It turns out that many of the practices related to location that we had previously understood as driven by some fundamental and underlying truth about how higher education works, were, in reality, merely practices that were determined by habit and tradition.

The most obvious change in how higher education is likely to think about place in the future has to do with staff, and specifically where staff work. While remote work may have been growing in pockets, possibly driven by high housing costs close to universities, working on campus was very much the norm. Many if not most schools had telework policies, but these were usually considered as exceptions, deviations from the norm of working on campus. While flexibility regarding where and when to get one's work done has long been a purview of faculty, staff were still expected to mostly show up physically. This idea, that productivity benefits from propinquity, was by no means limited to thinking about higher education staff. This was, prepandemic, a widely held belief across a range of industries and occupations. Just as the future of work in technology, finance, and media is likely to be more (maybe even majority) remote, so might we see a change in this basic assumption for academic staff. The current pandemic has revealed, to the great surprise of many, that productivity is a function of motivation and communication and technology and incentives and culture and a myriad of other factors, with location being only one of many considerations. In some cases, it may still be the most important consideration—staff working directly with students, for example—but it's not a given.

That said, it's entirely possible that we'll see as much of a push to return as many people as possible to campuses as can be accommodated. There are many advantages to be present with colleagues, from the serendipitous conversations that lead to productive work to the ability to manage difficult conversations and work habits in person. As with online learning, the jury has yet to yield a judgment in the value of teleworking for large numbers of college employees. At the very least, we know that campuses will be very different places if large swaths of academic staff work remotely. How other aspects of higher education's relationship to place will change once the pandemic passes are equally unclear. The biggest question mark for everyone in the online learning community is will COVID-19 accelerate or inhibit the growth of distance education? There are reasons to believe that both results are possible.

Looking at this question from where we are now, it is likely easier to make the case that the forced pivot to remote learning will end up setting back the perception that online learning is a destination that higher education should be aiming for. One thing we know we can say about remote learning is that it has been difficult for many of our students. How difficult?

This is yet unknown. Anecdotal evidence suggests that the number of students who faced considerable challenges succeeding in remotely taught courses will be high. Only after the survey results and data on student success and return rates are analyzed will we know how challenging things have been at schools across the country. To the extent that online education is tarnished by the remote learning brush, the image of online education will surely suffer.

On the other hand, what the COVID-19 emergency has shown some students and faculty is that online learning is not some mysterious practice. Given the right students, enough time, and the proper resources and assistance, online learners and educators can thrive together. Professors have at least caught glimpses of the connections that can be built with learners when communications are not limited by the few hours classes meet in a physical classroom but can extend to virtual communications on asynchronous discussion boards and synchronous online class meetings. Online courses, when designed well, can allow all students in a class (even the quiet ones) to have a voice. Faculty have seen that remote teaching is not perfect. But they have also been given an indication of how good online education could be, if only there was more time to prepare and more resources (like learning designers) to provide some help.

Where thinking about place is certain to change on the other end of the pandemic, whenever that should come, is around the affordances of face-to-face interactions. The gravitational pull of students and faculty back to campus may be strong (many staff will stay remote), but what is done on campus is likely to change. The emergency shift to remote learning has demonstrated both the value of social closeness (the opposite of social distancing), educational cohesiveness, and engagement as well as the reality that some things work very well when accomplished digitally.

For instance, time on campus may be seen as more precious, causing face-to-face interactions between learners and educators to receive greater care and attention in design and implementation. Tasks that can be moved to asynchronous online platforms, such as content delivery and assessment, likely will be. Office hours and advising appointments might shift to synchronous meeting platforms. Class time will be reserved more for interaction, collaboration, creating, and coaching.

None of these ideas are new, and indeed they have long been advocated for by educational developers and learning designers. Blended learning has long been thought of as an ideal. What will be new is that these practices might find much more widespread acceptance and adoption. COVID-19 certainly has highlighted the divide between residential and remote learning, with much more of the teaching and learning experience existing across modalities. The result may be that even after the pandemic has fully passed—meaning an effective vaccine is available and universally distributed—that the relationship between higher education and space will likely be permanently altered.

Learning

The third theme that has emerged for us in thinking about the future of higher education through the lens of the *15 Scenarios* framework has to do with learning. What COVID-19 has helped to clarify is that among all the activities in which colleges and universities engage, learning is at the very core. This is a theme that we explored at length in our book *Learning Innovation and the Future of Higher Education* and that we think the emergency pivot to remote education has brought sharply into focus.

Claiming that learning is central to the mission of colleges and universities might sound, on initial hearing, like stating the obvious. Of course, learning is what colleges and universities are all about. Who could argue with that? The reality is that while a focus on learning was never absent from every school, its centrality and prominence can vary significantly across institutions. While many colleges and universities hold dear to the mission to advance student learning, others tend to give it less weight (usually than research) in promotion and tenure.

Institutions of higher learning also have missions beyond that of advancing learning. These missions include the creation of knowledge, service to communities, accomplishments in athletics, and others. During the first months of COVID-19, the diversity of institutional missions were necessarily circumscribed, with most of the energy and resources of schools shifting to teaching and learning. The pandemic has catalyzed an all-hands-on-deck approach, with various parts of often decentralized organizations working together to ensure academic continuity in the form of remote learning.

This is not to argue that learning improved uniformly during the spring of 2020. The speed and the scale that schools needed to move from residential to remote education necessitated a more modest set of goals. In the emergency, keeping classes going was more important than advancing the state of the art of student learning. That said, many faculty took the opportunity to adapt to the new remote reality in ways that few could have predicted. The learning that went on in remote environments was complex, challenging, and exhausting for all involved, faculty and students alike. It required more time, more effort, and constant adjustments. As we've talked to colleagues across the country, we've heard stories of success and of challenge. The investment of effort required to teach remotely well may be one of the lasting lessons of this time.

To support this work, many campuses threw more resources into the process of developing and running courses—and of supporting students and faculty—than was customarily the case. Across the higher education ecosystem, teams that pre-COVID-19 were in charge of professional faculty development, online education, instructional design, educational technologies, and learning innovation were placed at the center of academic continuity efforts. Campus units that had worked on areas related to digital learning now found themselves at the center of institutional strategies for instructional resilience. Instructional designers and educational developers were more and more acknowledged as a necessity. Expertise in online education that may have resided in individual schools or programs, outside of the core residential undergraduate experience, was now in high demand across the campus. Nonfaculty educational staff, and the units that they work in, such as centers for teaching and learning (CTLs) and academic computing groups, came to be viewed as essential for the continuity of the institution.

How much of this rebalancing of priorities toward the educational mission will remain once the pandemic passes? As we move forward, the ability to rapidly shift between residential and online instruction may begin to be understood as a core competency. At many schools, faculty from across many different types of institutions have developed different working relationships with CTLs and academic computing units, just as staff who may previously have been one step removed from the teaching and learning enterprise were trained in the basic principles of course development and instructional design. Professors with interest or experience in online learning were often trained and deployed as peer mentors. All of this hard-won pedagogical experience and newly formed learning expertise will hopefully point to the possibility of greater investment in innovations in teaching and learning well after the pandemic subsides.

Perhaps more importantly, coronavirus has helped make visible the challenges of many of our students across the country. One effect has been the growing spread of the adoption of the idea of caring for the whole person (*cura personalis*, in the Jesuit tradition present at Georgetown University, where one of us teaches) across higher education and throughout all aspects of the campuses. An underappreciated aspect of teaching and learning during COVID-19 is the degree to which instructors and staff also filled in as coaches and mentors. Learning is very difficult in the best of times, and incredibly difficult when our students are anxious, stressed, and uncertain—conditions that are synonymous with life during a pandemic.

Throughout all this, faculty and staff have shown incredible care for their students, even while they have had to manage the unique circumstances of their own lives during this pandemic. Going forward, the experience of teaching during a national or world health crisis will likely cause many faculty to be more attuned and aware of the nonacademic challenges that their students face. An orientation toward a teaching approach that explicitly emphasizes the caring for and well-being of learners may outlive the pandemic. This altered relationship between professors and students may ultimately be the true teaching and learning legacy of COVID-19.

III. NEXT STEPS

Schools are making decisions. They've all been thinking about delivering academic and cocurricular programs, about finances, and about operations, all under the guidance of public health information and guidelines necessary to keep our communities safe. We've presented fifteen scenarios that we hope schools might consider as they make these decisions. Whatever decisions a school makes, however, one message all colleges and universities should embrace is that it's time to start preparing. This preparation comes in a lot of forms, from getting our residence halls ready for low-density occupation to organizing remote (or socially distanced) versions of the back-to-school and first-year student events that normally kick off the academic year to implementing protocols for testing, contact tracing, and potential quarantining of sick members of our campus communities. While the planning continues, we know we have a lot we need to do to get the members of our colleges and universities ready for teaching and learning under the continued presence of COVID-19.

This is particularly true when it comes to delivering the academic programming our students expect at our institutions. Whether we are on campus in some capacity, fully remote, or some hybrid, it is important for us to prepare to teach under what will no doubt be difficult external and internal circumstances. The situation with COVID-19 will require significant changes to how we engage and interact with each other. Our classrooms will look different. Our faculty, staff, and students will all likely continue to experience the stresses that come along with the ongoing pandemic. We need to prepare to support each other and to do the best work we can while navigating the impact of COVID-19.

This will not be easy. We spent much of the spring of the 2020 academic year, and the early part of that summer, thinking about how to move all of our courses to a remote learning environment. This involved little preparation beyond what schools may have done prior to develop institutional structures to support teaching excellence, learning innovation, or instructional continuity. This was a Herculean effort from faculty and staff across the country. We all worked on adrenaline and good will, resulting in some incredibly creative and thoughtful engagements. We had successes and we had challenges. Some things went very well, and some did not go as well.

We want to suggest that this current preparation involves two important streams. The first is helping faculty prepare to teach under conditions of continued social distancing, masks, and other constraints. This involves working with faculty to consider what it means to teach in whatever mode their schools decide they will be in when they return to campus. James DeVaney and Rebecca Quintana, of the University of Michigan, have written eloquently about proposed ways of thinking about resilient teaching.[22] Many schools are designing summer workshops and training. They are creating opportunities for faculty to learn in greater depth the tools they relied on in the spring. They are adding resources to websites and making the best pedagogical materials available to colleagues across their campuses and across the globe. The amount of energy and thinking and work being carried out by our educators and learning innovators is incredible. Students across the country will return to campuses with faculty who have embraced the need to make the teaching and learning experience as rich and as meaningful as possible given the circumstances.

The second stream is perhaps less obvious. It's not something we tend to give a lot of attention to in higher education. We need to prepare our students to be dynamic learners in whatever environment they find themselves in. We need to help them learn how to learn. We need to help them excel in a hybrid mode or in a fully remote environment. We need to give them the tools they need to succeed. And these tools are different from the skills they've developed for much of their education prior to college.

22. Rebecca Quintana and James DeVaney, "Laying the Foundation for a Resilient Teaching Community," *Inside Higher Ed*, May 27, 2020, https://www.insidehighered.com/blogs/learning-innovation/laying-foundation-resilient-teaching-community.

We spent time in this book speaking about the need to reach out to students. To help keep them connected to their colleges and universities over the summer. To bring them into their school's community for the first time if they are first-year students. We also need to communicate to them what they need to prepare. We should be reaching out to talk with them about expectations and to understand their challenges. We need to know what concerns they have and what accommodations they might need.

Just as getting our colleges and universities ready for the low-density university means preparing a complex operation and set of activities to make their transition to campus life possible, we need to help our students transition to the learning environment each of our schools will be designing. Teaching and learning during a world health emergency will be a challenging time for all of us. If we are going to be successful, we need to think about how we all adapt—faculty, staff, and students alike—to this new experience.

Acknowledgments

We'd like to thank the following colleagues, peers, and friends who generously gave of their expertise and time in contributing to our development of the scenarios for the low-density university outlined in this book: Derek Bruff, Adam Croom, Chris Dellarocas, James DeVaney, Kristen Eshleman, Jill Leafstedt, Rolin Moe, Mark Nemec, Matthew Rascoff, Matt Reed, Clay Shirky, Rebecca Stein, and Mary Wright.

Eddie would like to thank Sue Lorenson, Vice Dean for Undergraduate Education at Georgetown University, for providing feedback on a number of early drafts of the fifteen scenarios. Her insights helped shape much of the thinking of this book.